MANY MARRIAGES

by

Sherwood Anderson

A Critical Edition

edited by

Douglas G. Rogers

The Scarecrow Press, Inc.
Metuchen, N.J. & London
1978

Library of Congress Cataloging in Publication Data

Anderson, Sherwood, 1876-1941.
    Many marriages.

    I. Rogers, Douglas G., 1948-   II.   Title.
PZ3. A55Man   1978   [PS3501. N4]   813'.5'2   78-2353
ISBN 0-8108-1122-7

Manufactured in the United States of America

For
My parents,
Max and Gladys Rogers

TABLE OF CONTENTS

v

INTRODUCTION

Sherwood Anderson worked sporadically on the writing of Many Marriages for nearly three years. Early in 1920 and shortly after completing Poor White, Anderson wrote to Van Wyck Brooks: "Have begun a rollicking, Rabelaisian book called Many Marriages, a thing I have long hungered to do."[1] In July of that year, he wrote to his friends Jerome and Lucile Blum:

> In New York I got my new novel [Poor White] into the printer's hands. I'm deep in a new one called Many Marriages. There is an idea of a new novel form floating about in me, something looser, more real, more true. I want to go after that.[2]

In December, 1921, Anderson was awarded the first Dial prize of two thousand dollars. The award, created to provide a selected artist with financial freedom "to serve God (or go to the Devil) according to his own lights,"[3] enabled Anderson to assume residence in New Orleans, where he could more seriously pursue the writing of Many Marriages.

Anderson had also been working on a novel entitled Ohio Pagans, "a living tale, ... full of winds and barnyards and people."[4] By the time he arrived in New Orleans, he had written most of Ohio Pagans but, unsatisfied with it, "put it aside to mature more fully"[5] in himself and devoted his energies to Many Marriages.

In writing Many Marriages Anderson believed he had found a form that was most appropriate for the novel's content and a subject matter that would provide material for several novels. By late 1921, he was established as a fine writer of short stories but had been criticized for his seeming inability to manage longer, sustained narratives. None of his early novels--not Windy McPherson's Son, nor March-

ing Men, nor Poor White--was considered first-rate. At
times in these books he approached greatness, but ultimately
he wrote finely, never supremely.

However, in writing Winesburg, Ohio Anderson had
struck upon a medium more appropriate for his particular
writing skills. Reflecting on the writing of Winesburg, Anderson felt that taken together the Winesburg stories

> made something like a novel, a complete story....
> I have sometimes thought that the novel form does
> not fit an American writer, that it is a form which
> had been brought in. What is wanted is a new
> looseness; and in Winesburg I had made my own
> form. 6

Anderson constantly experimented with form. In March,
1921, he wrote to Paul Rosenfeld: "I can accept no standard
I have ever seen as to form. What I most want is to be
and remain always an experimenter, an adventurer."7

In January, 1922, Anderson wrote to his French
translator, Madame Gay:

> I have conceived of a form and a quick nervous
> prose that will have in it something of the intense
> nervousness of modern life while it, at the same
> time, strikes at what seems to me the diseases
> of modern life. 8

In early February, 1922, he wrote to his publisher,
Ben Huebsch, expressing uncertainty as to the nature of the
form he was creating: "The book ... will be a pretty long
one and I defy the gods to tell whether it is a novel or a
new way of handling and intermingling long short stories."9
Later that month, he again wrote to Huebsch, reiterating
concerns he had expressed to Madame Gay:

> I think the new prose is going to be unlike any-
> thing I've written. I am struggling to get a quick
> nervous rush to the thing, something internally
> suggestive of modern life. 10

While Anderson sought to bring a sense of the nervous rush of modern life to his prose, he was also feeling
the pressure of his second marriage collapsing. In the fall
of 1922, Anderson wrote to friends like Gertrude Stein that

he and Tennessee Mitchell "were not doing the job of being man and wife very well so we called it off."[11] In January, 1923, Anderson, already in love with Elizabeth Prahl, who was to become his third wife, wrote to Mrs. Hahn about his marriage to Tennessee:

> How did I know under what a cloud I lived. The central fact that T [Tennessee] is one who of herself cannot believe in life becomes more apparent.
> The dark moody terrible thing always lurking there. Poor child--I know she came toward me and toward something warm and in the end I grew tired and myself wanted warmth outside myself.[12]

Anderson perceived himself suffocating within his marriage and sought to escape from the heavy cloud beneath which he lived. He, like John Webster of Many Marriages, sought new life outside a sterile and meaningless marital relationship.

The disintegration of Anderson's second marriage no doubt influenced the thought that led to the writing of Many Marriages. In February, 1922, Anderson explained to Ben Huebsch:

> There is within every human being a deep well of thinking over which a heavy iron lid is kept clamped.
> Something tears the lid away. A kind of inner release takes place. In other words the man cuts sharply across all the machinery of the life about him. There is in the old Christian phrase a rebirth.
> Is this man in his new phase sane or insane. He does new things, says new and strange things and his words and actions fall with strange illuminating power on those about him. To some they are sentences of death, to others invitations into life.
> What I aim to do you see is to show step by step the process of this rebirth in a man and its effect on those about him.[13]

Having left Tennessee behind, and with the central thrust of Many Marriages clearly in mind, Anderson ventured to New Orleans to concentrate upon the writing of his book. He approached both his new novel and New Orleans enthusiastically. In a letter to Madame Gay, Anderson described living in the French Quarter:

> They have kept the old French town almost com-
> pletely intact and to this old town I have come to
> be alone, work, think and feel for a time. I have
> a large room with a fireplace and windows that go
> from the floor to the high old ceilings. By stepping
> out through the window I come upon a balcony,
> running the entire length of the old house and as
> wide as a city pavement, say of your Latin Quarter.
> Below me the life of the street goes on.
> Here I work and look at life. Then I go to
> write. [14]

The furnishings in Anderson's room included "a picture of the Virgin over the mantle and beside it two glass candle-sticks, in the form of crosses with Christs on the Cross in bronze on them."[15] Through Anderson's artistic imagination, the candlesticks and picture of the Virgin became part of the altar of life created by John Webster in his room in Many Marriages.

Anderson finally completed the novel in New Orleans and began to sort through the possibilities for publication. Ben Huebsch was contracted to publish the book version, but Anderson was also interested in magazine serialization. In earlier association with The Dial, Anderson had sought to serialize Poor White,[16] but the plan fell through because of the novel's length. The Dial had serialized the long story "Out of Nowhere into Nothing" in its July, August, and September issues in 1921. Serialization augmented Anderson's income, provided good publicity, and expanded his reading audience. He was, therefore, most receptive to an invitation from Gilbert Seldes, managing editor of The Dial, to send along the manuscript of Many Marriages for possible serialization beginning in the summer or fall of 1922.[17]

Correspondence with Seldes suggests that the original version of Many Marriages was too long for magazine pub-lication. In its May issue The Dial announced its intention to serialize Anderson's novel, but having made the announce-ment Seldes faced the dilemma of securing from Anderson a somewhat shortened manuscript. On April 21, 1922, he wrote to Anderson:

> Having announced that we are going to publish

this damned novel, what in God's name can we do?
(Excuse rough talk. Have been reading Ulysses.)
Now the thing for you to do is bring it down to
57,748 words, inaccurately speaking, and send it
to us and we will deal fairly with you. 18

In revising, Anderson shortened the novel and pointed
out to Seldes, "You will see that every undesirable citizen of
this corrupt city of my fancy has been jailed, sand-bagged,
thrown out of town."19 Thus, it would appear that Anderson
condensed his original manuscript of the novel for serialization in The Dial.

The Dial published Many Marriages in six segments
from October, 1922 until March, 1923. A longer book-length
version was published by Ben Huebsch in February, 1923.
Anderson affixed a short note to the Huebsch edition explaining his expansion of the novel:

I wish to make an explanation--that should perhaps
be also an apology--to the readers of The Dial.
To the magazine I make due acknowledgment
for the permission to print in this book form.
To The Dial reader I must explain that the
story has been greatly expanded since it appeared
serially in the magazine. The temptation to amplify my treatment of the theme was irresistible. If
I have succeeded in thus indulging myself without
detriment to my story I shall be glad. [Many
Marriages, "An Explanation"]

Anderson critics disagree about whether the book-
length version is, as Anderson stated in his "Explanation,"
an expansion of The Dial version or simply a publication of
the original manuscript as it stood prior to revision for
serialization. However, as Janis E. Cole skillfully argues
in her dissertation on Many Marriages, there is strong evi-
dence to suggest that Anderson had presented Huebsch with
a longer manuscript before sending a revised text to The
Dial.20 Anderson's correspondence with Huebsch supports
Dr. Cole's contention. At no point in the Newberry's collection of Anderson letters does he mention expanding The
Dial version for book publication.

When first released, Many Marriages was startling,
controversial, and wide-selling. The Huebsch hard-cover
edition sold for two dollars, and Anderson received a fifteen

per cent royalty (thirty cents per copy). Initial sales were strong, with Anderson receiving a royalty check of $2,758.50, representing 9,150 books, for the period from February until April 30th, 1923.[21]

F. Scott Fitzgerald hailed it as "the full-blown flower of Anderson's personality" and perceived the creation of John Webster as a "rather stupendous achievement."[22] Numerous critics, including Llewellyn Jones of the Chicago Evening Post, agreed with Fitzgerald and claimed that in "Many Marriages Mr. Anderson has attained the same success in a novel that in the past he has attained in short sketches; and indeed, this book is undoubtedly the best thing he has done so far."[23] But a strong reaction soon set in against the novel's subject matter, and sales sharply declined during the next six months; Anderson's royalties dropped for the period May 1st to October 31st to $306.20.

Critics such as the reviewer for the New York Times Book Review ridiculed Anderson for his seeming obsession with sex and nudity:

> The fact that most people do quite frequently take off their clothes, that every life may be said to have its unclad moments, though familiar enough to the majority of us, seems to strike Mr. Anderson as a new and remarkable phenomenon, which it is his solemn, even religious duty to proclaim aloud, continually and vociferously.[24]

Other critics, like H. W. Boynton, argued even more bluntly: "Many Marriages is a pretentious tract upon a trite theme, the slavery of the marriage bond."[25] Many among Anderson's reading public considered it immoral and obscene. Many libraries refused to buy it, and booksellers refused to display it on their shelves.

Anderson had anticipated the type of controversy his novel might arouse. In 1919, Winesburg, Ohio had created a similar stir. Though critical reception was much more favorable than Anderson ever admitted, some critics did condemn the book as dirty and its author as sex-obsessed. At the time, Anderson had defended himself and his Chicago contemporaries against their harshest critics:

> We had the notion that sex had something to do with people's lives, and it had barely been men-

tioned in American writing before our time. No
one it seemed ever used a profane word. And
bringing sex to take what seemed to us its normal
place in the picture of life, we were called sex-
obsessed. 26

At one point in his deliberations about publishing the
book, Anderson actually considered having it "printed in a
special limited edition, as the George Moore and Lawrence's
Women In Love have been done here."27

However, in a letter to Anderson, Ben Huebsch argued successfully against the limited edition, believing that
to

issue a book in that manner is to stamp it as
pornography. This new feature in book-selling has
resulted in the creation of a class known as book-
leggers. They sell books with a wink and a leer.
If the book happens to be a work of art they handle
it with slimy fingers. For you to bring out a book
in that manner means to limit its reading to one
or two thousand persons interested mainly in the
collector's value, or the obscenity value, and to
withhold it from your real audience, ninety-eight
per cent of which consists of people who can af-
ford to pay only the normal market price of
books. 28

The Huebsch edition stirred both moralistic and aes-
thetic controversy. On March 15, 1923, the New York
Times editorialized against several novels in an article entitled "Advertising Bad Books." Many Marriages was
amongst those cited:

The thing that makes one groan for American literature is the books--which may or may not be
immoral in Mr. Sumner's opinion--that make, and
are intended to make, an appeal to pretentious and
solemn minds.
Mr. Sherwood Anderson's latest is a case in
point. It contains passages which may seem to be
mere grotesque obscenity. Yet it is painfully apparent that Mr. Anderson thought he had a Message.
One can even see, dimly, what he is trying to get
over: a thought not devoid of merit, though far
from original. But because he is windy and ter-

ribly solemn he achieves something that looks like mere lasciviousness to some, while others who enjoy great repute as hierophants fall on their faces and do him reverence as the producer of something that must be great because it looks ridiculous.

If Mr. Sumner tries to suppress this book or others like it, he will merely bring a piece of pompous flatulence to the attention of people who will like it for the very reason that makes Sumner dislike it, and who will be as incapable as he of appreciating the real offense of Mr. Sherwood Anderson. Solemnity ought to be a misdemeanor and pretentiousness a felony. [29]

Perhaps even more alarming than the opinions of Mr. Sumner, an official of the New York Society for the Suppression of Vice, was the warning sounded by Dr. Bliss Perry, chairman of the English Department at Harvard University. In an address to the New England Watch and Ward Society, Dr. Perry warned:

Many book-lovers, neither prudish nor prurient in their tastes, have been shocked and bewildered by certain English and American novels in the last two years. High-minded publishers and booksellers have been perplexed as to their duty. Fathers and mothers and teachers have been troubled; and so have been librarians, and reviewers and many writers of books. In fact, no one whose professional work brings him into contact with the book-making, book-selling, and book-reading classes of the community can possibly be ignorant of the very general conviction that the American public is now facing a 'clear and present danger' through unclean books. [30]

Dr. Perry included Anderson amongst those writers whose works were unclean because of a preoccupation with sex.

Many critics defended Anderson's work against the charges of immorality and sexual obsession. Herbert J. Seligmann found Anderson's work clean and truthful:

It is the gospel of the body, the house people live in, he has been writing and in his pages is the fervor and wonder of one newly awakened to the possibilities of clarity and loveliness in others and in self. [31]

The reviewer in the Stanford Spectator felt that an unhealthy and outdated morality blinded many readers to the central message of Anderson's novel. Far from being immoral, Many Marriages championed the

> truth that there is no sacred love between man and woman which is dissociated from the physical senses, that man should not fear and hate his own body, but ought to recognize and admit with openness and respect, not with shame, its quality of being inviolable. [32]

Writing in The Bookman, Percy N. Stone wrote that "Sherwood Anderson has never written anything better," and suggested to his readers that although the subject matter may shock some, "we feel certain you will enjoy it immensely."[33]

The reviewer in the Binghamton Morning Sun argued that sensitive readers might be offended by Anderson's novel, but championed the artist's candor:

> Anderson writes starkly realistic facts, yet molds them with such beauty of words and with such never-failing cleanness of touch that to the wise reader they will be aesthetic inspiration rather than something at which to take offense. [34]

Anderson attempted to remain aloof from the critical debate, though the attacks on his artistic integrity were painful. In a letter to Paul Rosenfeld shortly after the publication of Poor White (1920), Anderson wrote of his fears about sharing a work of art with the public:

> I have just published a book myself and that always means for me a period of mental illness. One is building a house which he does build with love. On a certain day he opens the door and going into the street invites the people to enter. Inspite of himself he does in some vague, foolish way, expect all the people to come joyously, to understand against what difficulties he has struggled.
>   They don't at all. Most of them are engaged in house building ... of their own. One finds ... he has been dreaming of some impossible brotherhood of understanding. [35]

The quote applies well to the reception of Many Marriages. Though Anderson's novel had many admirers, its detractors and a strong censorship lobby worked against popular reception. Many Marriages has been republished only once since its initial appearance in 1923 (Grosset and Dunlap, 1928). Relegated to critical oblivion, it remains one of Anderson's most misunderstood and grossly neglected books.

In compiling a critical edition of Many Marriages, I wanted to note all textual variations but also to provide a highly readable text. Consequently, I have reprinted the first Ben Huebsch edition exactly as it appeared in 1923. Textual variations are noted with asterisks (*) and are listed in the appendix.

In researching the text, I had available to me no fewer than four stages of Anderson's work: 1) the Dial version published serially from October, 1922 through March, 1923; 2) a 148-typed page manuscript (housed at the Newberry Library in Chicago) with notes by Anderson and the printer and red pencil marks by J.D.C. who reported on the manuscript to its purchaser, Mr. Burton Emmett, on June 24, 1929. The manuscript appears to be a fair copy of The Dial magazine version; 3) the first book-length printing of the novel by Ben Huebsch in February, 1923; and 4) a 168-page manuscript (also housed at the Newberry) consisting of pages and partial pages of pica and elite typing and galley sheets, and with editorial notes by both Anderson and the printer. This appears to be the fair copy for the Huebsch edition.

Careful comparison of the four versions of the text has yielded hundreds of textual variations including changes of punctuation, printing errors, spelling variations (The Dial editors preferred the English spellings for such words as "colour" and "grey" and "parlour"), and inclusion or deletion of phrases, whole sentences, and whole paragraphs. The Huebsch edition, substantially longer than the magazine version, incorporates whole paragraphs omitted in The Dial. Most importantly, of course, Anderson omitted an entire book, Book IV, from the serialized text.

In general, changes made by Anderson are typed or handwritten in the manuscripts in blue, green, or black ink. Printer's changes--most often, spelling or punctuation--are written or printed in pencil.

NOTES

[1]Howard Mumford Jones and Walter B. Rideout, ed., The Letters of Sherwood Anderson (Boston: Little, Brown, and Co., 1953), letter #46. p. 55.

[2]Ibid., letter #48, p. 58.

[3]"Announcement," The Dial, 70 (June 1921), p. 731.

[4]Jones and Rideout, letter #49, p. 60.

[5]Sherwood Anderson, Letter to Ben Huebsch, 3 February 1922, Newberry Library's Anderson Collection (hereafter abbreviated N.L.A.C.).

[6]Sherwood Anderson, Sherwood Anderson's Memoirs (New York: Harcourt, Brace, and Co., 1942).

[7]Jones and Rideout, letter #59, p. 72.

[8]Sherwood Anderson, Letter to Madame Gay, January 1922, N.L.A.C.

[9]Sherwood Anderson, Letter to Ben Huebsch, 3 February 1922, N.L.A.C.

[10]Sherwood Anderson, Letter to Ben Huebsch, 17 February 1922, N.L.A.C.

[11]Sherwood Anderson/Gertrude Stein: Correspondence and Personal Essays, Ray Lewis White, ed. (Chapel Hill: University of North Carolina, 1972), p. 22.

[12]Sherwood Anderson, Letter to Mrs. Virginia Hahn, January 1923, N.L.A.C.

[13]Sherwood Anderson, Letter to Ben Huebsch, February 1922, N.L.A.C.

[14]Sherwood Anderson, Letter to Madame Gay, 19 January 1922, N.L.A.C.

[15]Sherwood Anderson, Letter to Jerome Blum, 2 February 1922, N.L.A.C.

[16]See letter written to Anderson by Scofield Thayer, editor of The Dial, 17 July 1920, N.L.A.C.

[17]See letter written to Anderson by Gilbert Seldes, managing editor of The Dial, 9 March 1922, N.L.A.C.

[18]Gilbert Seldes, Letter to Sherwood Anderson, 21 April 1922, N.L.A.C.

[19]Sherwood Anderson, Letter to Gilbert Seldes, 24 April 1922, N.L.A.C.

[20]Janis E. Cole, "Many Marriages: Sherwood Anderson's Controversial Novel," Dissertation, University of Michigan, 1965.

[21]See royalties statements in folder marked "Huebsch, B. W., Inc.", N.L.A.C.

[22]F. Scott Fitzgerald, "Sherwood Anderson on the Marriage Question," New York Herald, 4 March 1923, sec. 9, p. 5.

[23]Llewellyn Jones, "Sherwood Anderson's Biggest Achievement," Chicago Evening Post Literary Review, 2 March 1923.

[24]New York Times Book Review, 25 February 1923, p. 10.

[25]H. W. Boynton, "Man the Blunderer," Independent, 110 (31 March 1923), p. 23.

[26]Sherwood Anderson, "Anderson on Winesburg, Ohio," Winesburg, Ohio: Text and Criticism, ed. John H. Ferres (New York: Viking Press, 1966), p. 17.

[27]Sherwood Anderson, Letter to Ben Huebsch, 2 February 1922, N.L.A.C.

[28]Ben Huebsch, Letter to Sherwood Anderson, 11 February 1922, N.L.A.C.

[29]"Advertising Bad Books," New York Times, 15 March 1923, Sec. 1, p. 18.

[30]Bliss Perry, "Address on Pernicious Books," Forty-Fifth Annual Report of the New England Watch and Ward Society, 1922-23 (Boston, 1923), pp. 20-21.

[31]Herbert J. Seligmann, M.S.S. (The Tin Whistle) or Rejected by the Orchestra, March 1923, p. 3.

[32]C. W. "Many Marriages: Sherwood Anderson," Stanford Spectator, June 1923.

[33]Percy N. Stone, "Novels a la Carte," The Bookman, 57 (April 1923), p. 211.

[34]Binghamton (New York) Morning Sun, 14 June 1923.

[35]Jones and Rideout, letter #54, pp. 65-66.

CHRONOLOGY

1876   September 13: born the third of seven children to Irwin and Emma Anderson in Camden, Ohio.

1884   Family settles in Clyde, Ohio, a town which later serves as semi-prototype for Winesburg.

1895   Serves in Company I, 16th Infantry of the Ohio National Guard. Anderson's mother, Emma, dies of consumption.

1896   Leaves Clyde to work in an apple warehouse in Chicago.

1898   Serves in Company I, Sixth Ohio Regiment of Volunteer Infantry, during Spanish-American War.

1900   June: graduates from Wittenberg Academy, Springfield, Ohio. Returns to Chicago; writes and sells advertising copy for the Crowell Publishing Company.

1904   May 16: marries Cornelia Lane in Toledo, Ohio.

1906   Assumes presidency of the United Factories Company in Cleveland, Ohio.

1907   August 16: first son, Robert, born. Starts a mail-order paint firm in Elyria, Ohio.

1908   The successful Anderson Manufacturing Company begins producing its own paint. December 31: second son, John, born.

1911   October 29: daughter, Marion, born.

1912   Writes early drafts of Windy McPherson's Son and Marching Men. December 1: found dazed and suffering from nervous exhaustion in Cleveland, Ohio.

1913   Leaves presidency of Anderson Manufacturing Company; returns to work for Taylor-Critchfield Advertising Company in Chicago.

1914   July: first short story: "The Rabbit-Pen."

1915   Divorces Cornelia Lane. December: "Sister" appears in Little Review.

1916   Windy McPherson's Son, first novel. Several of the Winesburg tales published: "The Book of the Grotesque," "Hands," and "The Strength of God" in Masses; "Paper Pills" in Little Review; "Queer" in The Seven Arts. Marries Tennessee Mitchell.

1917   Marching Men. Three Winesburg tales published: "The Untold Lie," "Mother," and "The Thinker" in The Seven Arts.

1918   Mid-American Chants. Two Winesburg tales published: "The Man of Ideas" and "An Awakening" in Little Review.

1919   Winesburg, Ohio.

1920   Poor White. Irwin Anderson, Sherwood's father, dies.

1921   The Triumph of the Egg. Wins Dial Award of two thousand dollars.

1923   Many Marriages. Horses and Men.

1924   A Story Teller's Story. Divorces Tennessee Mitchell. Marries Elizabeth Prall.

1925   The Modern Writer. Dark Laughter.

1926   Sherwood Anderson's Notebook. Tar: A Midwest Childhood. Purchases Ripshin Farm in Troutdale, Virginia.

1927   A New Testament. Buys two Marion, Virginia newspapers: Smyth County News and Marion Democrat.

1929   Alice and the Lost Novel. Hello Towns! Nearer the Grass Roots. Separates from Elizabeth Prall.

1930   The American County Fair.

1931   Perhaps Women.

1932   Beyond Desire. Divorces Elizabeth Prall. Attends
        "World's Congress Against War" in Amsterdam.

1933   Death in the Woods and Other Stories. July: Mar-
        ries Eleanor Copenhaver.

1934   No Swank. First dramatic presentation of Wines-
        burg, Ohio at the Hedgrow Theatre.

1935   Puzzled America.

1936   Kit Brandon.

1937   Plays: Winesburg and Others (Includes three one-
        act plays: The Triumph of the Egg, Mother, and
        They Married Later).

1939   A Writer's Conception of Realism, the text of an
        address delivered on January 20, 1939, at Olivet
        College in Olivet, Michigan. Five Poems.

1940   Home Town.

1941   March 8: dies of peritonitis in Colon, Panama Can-
        al Zone, while engaged in a State Department-pro-
        moted goodwill tour of South America.

1942   Sherwood Anderson's Memoirs.

1969   Sherwood Anderson's Memoirs: A Critical Edition,
        edited by Ray Lewis White.

1975   The Writer's Book: A Critical Edition, edited by
        Martha Mulroy Curry.

ACKNOWLEDGMENTS

In compiling a work of this type, one enters the debt of many individuals and institutions. I am particularly grateful to the Newberry Library and its excellent staff for a resident fellowship which enabled me to complete my research on the manuscripts in the Anderson Collection. I wish also to thank the highly professional and capable staffs of the University of Chicago Regenstein and Loyola University of Chicago Libraries. A number of colleagues offered valuable advice and information. I especially thank Dr. David D. Anderson of Michigan State University, Dr. Ray Lewis White of Illinois State University, Dr. William Veeder, and Dr. James E. Miller, Jr. of the University of Chicago. I am most grateful to Dr. Janis E. Cole for her penetrating research in an unpublished dissertation, "Many Marriages: Sherwood Anderson's Controversial Novel" and to Sally Rogers for her assistance in typing and proofing. Finally, I thank Mrs. Eleanor Copenhaver Anderson whose kindness and generosity made this critical edition possible.

The Text of
MANY MARRIAGES

SHERWOOD ANDERSON

MANY MARRIAGES

NEW YORK   B. W. HUEBSCH, Inc.   MCMXXIII

To
PAUL ROSENFELD

AN EXPLANATION*

I wish to make an explanation—that should perhaps be also an apology—to the readers of the *Dial*.

To the magazine I make due acknowledgment for the permission to print in this book form.

To the *Dial* reader I must explain that the story has been greatly expanded since it appeared serially in the magazine. The temptation to amplify my treatment of the theme was irresistible. If I have succeeded in thus indulging myself without detriment to my story I shall be glad.

SHERWOOD ANDERSON.

A FOREWORD

If one seek love and go towards it directly, or as directly as one may in the midst of the perplexities of modern life, one is perhaps insane.

Have you not known a moment when to do what would seem at other times and under somewhat different circumstances the most trivial of acts becomes suddenly a gigantic undertaking.

You are in the hallway of a house. Before you is a closed door and beyond the door, sitting in a chair by a window, is a man or woman.

It is late in the afternoon of a summer day and your purpose is to step to the door, open it, and say, "It is not my intention to continue living in this house. My trunk is packed and in an hour a man, to whom I have already spoken, will come for it. I have only come to say that I will not be able to live near you any longer."

There you are, you see, standing in the hallway, and you are to go into the room and say these few words. The house is silent and you stand for a long time in the hallway, afraid, hesitant, silent. In a dim way you realize that when you came down into the hallway from the floor above you came a-tiptoe.

For you and the one beyond the door it is perhaps better that you do not continue living in the house. On that you would agree if you could but talk sanely of the matter. Why are you unable to talk sanely?

Why has it become so difficult for you to take the three steps towards the door? You have no disease of the legs. Why are your feet so heavy?

You are a young man. Why do your hands tremble like the hands of an old man?

You have always thought of yourself as a man of courage. Why are you suddenly so lacking in courage?

Is it amusing or tragic that you know you will be unable to step to the door, open it, and going inside say the few words, without your voice trembling?

Are you sane or are you insane? Why this whirlpool of thoughts within your brain, a whirlpool of thoughts that, as you now stand hesitant, seem to be sucking you down and down into a bottomless pit?

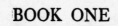

BOOK ONE

MANY MARRIAGES

I

THERE was a man named Webster lived in a town of twenty-five thousand people in the state of Wisconsin. He had a wife named Mary and a daughter named Jane and he was himself a fairly prosperous manufacturer of washing machines. When the thing happened of which I am about to write he was thirty-seven or eight years old and his one child, the daughter, was seventeen. Of the details of his life up to the time a certain revolution happened within him it will be unnecessary to speak. He was however a rather quiet man inclined to have dreams which he tried to crush out of himself in order that he function as a washing machine manufacturer; and no doubt, at odd moments, when he was on a train going some place or perhaps on Sunday afternoons in the summer when he went alone to the deserted office of the factory and sat for several hours looking out through a window and along a railroad track, he gave way to dreams.

However for many years he went quietly along his way doing his work like any other small manufacturer. Now and then he had a prosperous year

3

when money seemed plentiful and then he had bad years when the local banks threatened to close him up, but as a manufacturer he did manage to survive.

And so there was this Webster, drawing near to his fortieth year, and his daughter had just graduated from the town high school. It was early fall and he seemed to be going along and living his life about as usual and then this thing happened to him.

Down within his body something began to affect him like an illness. It is a little hard to describe the feeling he had. It was as though something were being born. Had he been a woman he might have suspected he had suddenly become pregnant. There he sat in his office at work or walked about in the streets of his town and he had the most amazing feeling of not being himself, but something new and quite strange. Sometimes the feeling of not being himself became so strong in him that he stopped suddenly in the streets and stood looking and listening. He was, let us say, standing before a small store on a side street. Beyond there was a vacant lot in which a tree grew and under the tree stood an old work horse.

Had the horse come down to the fence and talked to him, had the tree raised one of its heavier lower branches and thrown him a kiss or had a sign that hung over the store suddenly shouted saying—"John Webster, go prepare thyself for the day of the coming of God"—his life at that time would not have seemed more strange than it did. Nothing that could have happened in the exterior world, in the world of such hard facts as sidewalks under his feet, clothes on his body, engines pulling trains along the railroad tracks beside his factory, and street cars rumbling through the streets where he stood, none of these could possibly have done anything more amazing than the things that were at that moment going on within him.

There he was, you see, a man of the medium height, with slightly graying black hair, broad shoulders, large hands, and a full, somewhat sad and perhaps sensual face, and he was much given to the habit of smoking cigarettes. At the time of which I am speaking he found it very hard to sit still in one spot and to do his work and so he continually moved about. Getting quickly up from his chair in the factory office he went out into the shops. To do so he had to pass through a large outer office where there was a bookkeeper, a desk for his factory superintendent and other desks for three girls who also did some kind of office work, sent out circulars regarding the washing machine to possible buyers, and attended to other details.

In his own office there was a broad-faced woman of twenty-four who was his secretary. She had a strong, well-made body, but was not very handsome. Nature had given her a broad flat face and thick lips, but her skin was very clear and she had very clear fine eyes.

A thousand times, since he had become a manufacturer, John Webster had walked thus out of his

5

own office into the general office of the factory and out through a door and along a board walk to the factory itself, but not as he now walked.

Well,[*] he had suddenly begun walking in a new world, that was a fact that could not be denied. An idea came to him. "Perhaps I am becoming for some reason a little insane," he thought. The thought did not alarm him. It was almost pleasing. "I like myself better as I am now," he concluded.

He was about to pass out of his small inner office into the larger office and then on into the factory, but stopped by the door. The woman who worked there in the room with him was named Natalie Swartz. She was the daughter of a German saloon-keeper of the town who had married an Irish woman and then had died leaving no money. He remembered what he had heard of her and her life. There were two daughters and the mother had an ugly temper and was given to drink. The older daughter had become a teacher in the town schools and Natalie had learned stenography and had come to work in the office of the factory. They lived in a small frame house at the edge of town and sometimes the old mother got drunk and abused the two girls. They were good girls and worked hard, but in her cups the old mother accused them of all sorts of immorality. All the neighbors felt sorry for them.

John Webster stood at the door with the door-knob in his hand. He was looking hard at Natalie, but did not feel in the least embarrassed nor strangely enough did she. She was arranging some

6

papers, but stopped working and looked directly at him. It was an odd sensation to be able to look thus, directly into another person's eyes. It was as though Natalie were a house and he were looking in through a window. Natalie herself lived within the house that was her body. What a quiet strong dear person she was and how strange it was that he had been able to sit near her every day for two or three years without ever before thinking of looking into her house. "How many houses there are within which I have not looked," he thought.

A strange rapid little circle of thought welled up within him as he stood thus, without embarrassment, looking into Natalie's eyes. How clean she had kept her house. The old Irish mother in her cups might shout and rave calling her daughter a whore, as she sometimes did, but her words did not penetrate into the house of Natalie. The little thoughts within John Webster became words, not expressed aloud, but words that ran like voices shouting softly within himself. "She is my beloved," one of the voices said. "You shall go into the house of Natalie," said another. A slow blush spread over Natalie's face and she smiled. "You are not very well lately. Are you worried about something?" she said. She had never spoken to him before with just that manner.* There was a suggestion of intimacy about it. As a matter of fact the washing machine business was at that time doing very well. Orders were coming in rapidly and the factory was humming with life. There were no notes to be paid at the bank. "Why, I am

7

very well," he said, "very happy and very well, at just this moment."

He went on into the outer office and the three women employed there and the bookkeeper too stopped working to look at him. Their looking up from their desks was just a kind of gesture. They meant nothing by it. The bookkeeper came and asked a question regarding some account. "Why, I would like it if you would use your own judgment* about that," John Webster said. He was vaguely conscious the question had been concerned with some man's credit. Some man, in a far-away place had written to order twenty-four washing machines. He would sell them in a store. The question was, when the time came, would he pay the manufacturer?

The whole structure of business, the thing in which all the men and women in America were, like himself, in some way involved, was an odd affair. Really he had not thought much about it. His father had owned this factory and had died. He had not wanted to be a manufacturer. What had he wanted to be? His father had certain things called patents. Then the son, that was himself, was grown and had begun to manage the factory. He got married and after a time his mother died. Then the factory belonged to him. He made the washing machines that were intended to take the dirt out of people's clothes and employed men to make them and other men to go forth and sell them. He stood in the outer office seeing, for the first time, all life of modern men as a strange involved thing.

8

"It wants understanding and a lot of thinking about," he said aloud. The bookkeeper had turned to go back to his desk, but stopped and turned, thinking he had been spoken to. Near where John Webster stood a woman was addressing circulars. She looked up and smiled suddenly and he liked her smiling so. "There is a way—something happens—people suddenly and unexpectedly come close to each other," he thought and went out through the door and along the board walk toward the factory.

In the factory there was a kind of singing noise going on and there was a sweet smell. Great piles of cut boards lay about and the singing noise was made by saws cutting the boards into proper lengths and shapes to make up the parts of the washing machines. Outside the factory doors were three cars loaded with lumber and workmen were unloading boards and sliding them along a kind of runway into the building.

* John Webster felt very much alive. The timbers had no doubt come to his factory from a great distance. That was a strange and interesting fact. Formerly, in his father's time, there had been a great deal of timber land in Wisconsin but now the forests were pretty much cut away and timber was shipped in from the South. Somewhere, in the place from which had come the boards, now being unloaded at his factory door, were forests and rivers and men going into the forests and cutting down trees.

He had not for years felt so alive as he did at

9

that moment, standing there by the factory door and seeing the men slide the boards from the car along the runway and into the building. How peaceful and quiet the scene!* The sun was shining and the boards were of a bright yellow color. A kind of perfume came from them. His own mind was an amazing thing too. At the moment he could see, not only the cars and the men unloading them, but also the land from which the boards came. There was a place, far in the South, where the waters of a low marshy river had spread out until the river was two or three miles wide. It was spring and there had been a flood. At any rate, in the imagined scene, many trees were submerged and there were men in boats, black men, who were pushing logs out of the submerged forest into the wide sluggish stream. The men were great powerful fellows and sang as they worked, a song about John, the disciple and close comrade of Jesus. The men had on high boots and in their hands were long poles. Those in the boats on the river itself caught the logs when they were pushed out from among the trees and gathered them together to form a great raft. Two of the men jumped out of the boats and ran about on the floating logs fastening them together with young saplings. The other men, back somewhere in the forest, kept singing and the men on the raft answered. The song was about John and how he went down to fish in a lake. And the Christ came to call him and his brothers out of the boats to go through the hot dusty land of Galilee, "following in the footsteps of the Lord." Presently the song stopped and there was silence.

How strong and rhythmical the bodies of the workers!* Their bodies swayed back and forth as they worked. There was a kind of dance in their bodies.

Now two things happened in John Webster's fanciful world. A woman, a golden-brown woman, came down along the river in a boat and all the workmen stopped working to stand looking at her. She had no hat on her head and as she pushed the boat forward through the sluggish water her young body swayed from side to side, as the bodies of the men workers had swayed when they handled the logs. The hot sun was shining on the body of the brown girl and her neck and shoulders were bare. One of the men on the raft called to her. "Hello, Elizabeth," he shouted. She stopped paddling the boat and let it float for a moment.

"Hello you' self, you China boy," she answered laughing.

Again she began to paddle vigorously. A log shot out from amid the trees at the river's edge, the trees that were submerged in the yellow water, and a young black stood astride it. With the pole in his hand he gave a vigorous push against one of the trees and the log came swiftly down toward the raft where two other men stood waiting.

The sun was shining on the neck and shoulders of the brown girl in the boat. The movements of her arms made dancing lights on her skin. The skin was brown, a golden coppery brown. Her boat slipped about a bend of the river and disappeared. There was a moment of silence and then, from back among the trees, a voice took up a new song in which the other blacks joined—

"Doubting Thomas, doubting Thomas,
Doubting Thomas, doubt no more.

And before I'd be a slave,
I'd be buried in my grave,
And go home to my father and be saved."

John Webster stood with blinking eyes watching the men unload boards at his factory door. The little voices within him were saying strange joyous things.* One could not be just a manufacturer of washing machines in a Wisconsin town. In spite of oneself one became, at odd moments, something else too. One became a part of something as broad as the land in which one lived. One went about in a little shop in a town. The shop was in an obscure place, by a railroad track and beside a shallow stream, but it was also a part of some vast thing no one had as yet begun to understand. He himself was a man standing, clad in ordinary clothes, but within his clothes, and within his body too there was something, well perhaps not vast in itself, but vaguely indefinitely connected with some vast thing. It was odd he had never thought of that before. Had he thought of it? There were the men before him unloading the timbers. They touched the tim-

12

bers with their hands. A kind of union was made between them and the black men who had cut the timbers and floated them down a stream to a saw-mill in some far-away Southern place. One went about all day and every day touching things other men had touched. There was something wanted, a consciousness of the thing touched. A consciousness of the significance of things and people.

> "And before I'd be a slave,
> I'd be buried in my grave,
> And go home to my father and be saved."

He went through the door into his shop. Near by, at a machine, a man was sawing boards. There was no doubt the pieces selected for the making of his washing machine were not always of the best. Some of the pieces would soon enough break. They were put into a part of the machine where it didn't so much matter, where they wouldn't be seen. The machines had to be sold at a low price. He felt a little ashamed and then laughed. One might easily become involved in small things when there were big rich things to be thought about. One was a child and had to learn to walk. What was it one had to learn? To walk about smelling things, tasting things, feeling things perhaps. One had to learn who else was in the world besides one-self, for one thing. One had to look about a little. It was all very well to be thinking that better boards should be put into washing machines that* poor women bought, but one might easily become cor-

13

rupted by giving oneself*over to such thoughts. There was danger of a kind of smug self-righteousness got from thinking about putting only good boards in washing machines. He had known men like that and had always had a kind of contempt for them.

He went on through the factory, past rows of men and boys standing at machines at work, forming the various parts of the washing machines, putting the parts together, painting and packing the machines for shipment. The upper part of the building was given over to the storage of materials. He walked through piles of cut boards to a window that looked down upon the shallow and now half-dry stream on the banks of which the factory stood. There were signs all about forbidding smoking in the factory, but he had forgotten and now took a cigarette out of his pocket and lighted it.

A rhythm of thought went on within him*that was in some way related to the rhythm of the bodies of the black men at work in the forest of the world of his imagination. He had been standing before his factory door in a town in the state of Wisconsin but at the same time he was in the South, with some blacks working on a river, and at the same time with some fishermen on the shore of the Sea of Galilee, when a man came down to the shore and began to say strange words. "There must be more than one of me," he thought vaguely and when his mind had formed the thought something seemed to have happened within himself. A few moments before, as he stood in the presence of Natalie Swartz

14

down in the office, he had thought of her body as a house within which she lived. That was an illuminating thought too. Why could not more than one person live within such a house?

It would clear a good many things up if such an idea got abroad. No doubt it was an idea that had come to a great many other men, but perhaps they had not put it forth in a simple enough way. He had himself gone to school in his town and later to the University at Madison. For a time he had read a good many books. At one time he had thought he might like to be a writer of books.

And no doubt a great many of the writers of books had been visited by just such thoughts as he was having now. Within the pages of some books one found a kind of refuge from the tangle of things in daily life. Perhaps as they wrote, these men felt, as he felt now, exhilarated, carried out of themselves.

He puffed at his cigarette and looked beyond the river. His factory was at the edge of town and beyond the river fields began. All men and women were like himself standing on a common ground. All over America, all over the world for that matter, men and women did outward things much as he did. They ate food, slept, worked, made love.

He was growing a little weary of thinking and rubbed his hand across his forehead. His cigarette had burned out and he dropped it on the floor and lighted another. Men and women tried to go within one another's bodies, were at times almost insanely anxious to do it. That was called making love. He wondered if a time might come when men and women did that quite freely. It was difficult to try to think one's way through such a tangle of thoughts.

There was one thing sure, he had never before been in this state. Well that was not true. There was a time once. It was when he married. Then he had felt as he did now, but something had happened.

He began to think of Natalie Swartz. There was something clear and innocent about her. Perhaps, without knowing, he had fallen in love with her, the daughter of a saloon-keeper and the drunken old Irish woman. That would explain much* if it had happened.

He became aware of a man standing near him and turned. A workman in overalls stood a few feet away. He smiled. "I guess you have forgotten something," he said. John Webster smiled also. "Well yes," he said, "a good many things. I'm nearly forty years old and I guess I have forgotten to live. What about you?"

The workman smiled again. "I mean the cigarettes," he said and pointed to the burning and smoking end of the cigarette that lay on the floor. John Webster put his foot on it and then dropping the other cigarette to the floor put his foot on that. He and the workman stood looking at each other as but a little while before he had looked at Natalie Swartz. "I wonder if I might go within his house also," he thought. "Well, I thank you. I had forgotten. My mind was far away," he said aloud. The workman nodded. "I am sometimes like that myself," he explained.*

The puzzled manufacturer went down out of the upstairs room and along a branch of the railroad that led into the shop to the main tracks along which he walked toward the more inhabited part of town. "It must be almost noon," he thought. Usually he had lunch at a place near his factory and his employees brought their lunches in packages and tin pails. He thought now he would go to his own home. He would not be expected but thought he would like to look at his wife and daughter. A passenger train came rushing down along the tracks and although the whistle blew madly he was unaware of it. Then when it was almost upon him a young negro, a tramp perhaps, at any rate a black man in ragged clothes who was also walking on the tracks, ran to him and taking hold of his coat jerked him violently to one side. The train rushed past and he stood staring after it. He and the young negro also looked into each other's eyes. He put his hand into his pocket, instinctively feeling that he should pay the man for the service done him.

And then a kind of shudder ran through his body. He was very tired. "My mind was far away," he said. "Yes, boss. I'm sometimes that way myself," the young negro said, smiling and walking away along the tracks.

II

JOHN WEBSTER rode to his house on a street car. It was half-past twelve o'clock when he arrived and, as he had anticipated, he was not expected. Behind his house, a rather commonplace looking frame affair, there was a little garden with two apple trees. He walked around the house and saw his daughter, Jane Webster, lying in a hammock hung between the trees. There was an old rocking-chair under one of the trees near the hammock and he went and sat in it. His daughter was surprised at his coming upon her so, at the noon hour when he so seldom appeared. "Well, hello Dad," she said listlessly, sitting up and dropping on the grass at his feet a book she had been reading.* "Is there anything wrong?" she asked. He shook his head.

Picking up the book he began to read and her head dropped again to the cushion in the hammock. The book was a modern novel of the period. It concerned life in the old city of New Orleans. He read a few pages. It was no doubt the sort of thing that might take one out of oneself, take one away from the dullness*of life. A young man was stealing along a street in the darkness and had a cloak wrapped about his shoulders. Overhead the moon shone. The magnolia trees were in blossom filling the air with perfume. The young man was very handsome. The scene of the novel was laid in the time before the Civil War and he owned a great many slaves.

John Webster closed the book. There was no need of reading. When he was still a young man he had sometimes read such books himself. They took one out of oneself, made the dullness of everyday existence seem less terrible.

That was an odd thought, that everyday existence need be dull. There was no doubt the last twenty years of his own life had been dull, but during that morning, life had not been so. It seemed to him he had never before had such a morning.*

Another book lay in the hammock* and he took it* up and read a few lines:*

"You see," said Wilberforce calmly, 'I am returning to South Africa soon. I am not even planning to cast my fortunes with Virginia."

Umbrage broke into protestations, came up, and put his hand on John's arm, and then Malloy looked at his daughter. As he feared would be the case, her eyes were fastened on Charles Wilberforce. He had thought, when he brought her to Richmond that night, that she was looking wonderfully well and gay. So indeed she had been, with the prospect before her of seeing Charles again after six weeks. Now she was lifeless and pale as a candle from which the flame has been struck.

John Webster glanced at his daughter. As he sat he could look directly into her face.

"As pale as a candle from which the flame has

19

been struck, huh. What a fancy way of putting things." Well, his own daughter Jane was not pale. She was a robust young thing. "A candle that has never been lighted," he thought.

It was a strange and terrible fact, but the truth was he had never thought much about his daughter, and here she was almost a woman. There was no doubt she already had the body of a woman. The functions of womanhood went on in her body. He sat, looking directly at her. A moment before he had been very weary, now the weariness was quite gone. "She might already have had a child," he thought. Her body was prepared for child-bearing, it had grown and developed to that state.*
What an immature face she had. Her mouth was pretty but there was something, a kind of blankness. "Her face is like a fair sheet of paper on which nothing has been written."*
*Her eyes in wandering*met his eyes. It was odd. Something like fright came into them. She sat quickly up. "What's the matter with you, Dad?" she asked sharply. He smiled. "There isn't anything the matter," he said, looking away. "I thought I'd come home to lunch. Is there anything wrong about that?"

His wife, Mary Webster, came to the back door of the house and called her daughter. When she saw her husband her eyebrows went up. "This is unexpected. What brought you home at this time of the day?" she asked.

They went into the house and along a hallway to

20

the dining room, but there was no place set for him. He had a feeling they both thought there was something wrong, almost immoral, about his being home at that time of the day. It was unexpected and the unexpected has a doubtful air. He concluded he had better explain. "I had a headache and thought I would come home and lie down for an hour," he said. He felt they looked relieved, as though he had taken a load off their minds, and smiled at the thought. "May I have a cup of tea? Will it be too much trouble?" he asked.

While the tea was being brought he pretended to look out through a window, but in secret studied his wife's face. She was like her daughter. There was nothing written on her face. Her body was getting heavy.

She had been a tall slender girl with yellow hair when he married her. Now the impression she gave off was of one who had grown large without purpose, "somewhat as cattle are fattened for slaughter," he thought. One did not feel the bone and muscle back of her bulk. Her yellow hair that, when she was younger, had a way of glistening strangely in the sunlight was now rather colorless.* It had the air of being dead at the roots and there were folds of quite meaningless flesh on the face among which little streams of wrinkles wandered.

"Her face is a blank thing, untouched by the finger of life," he thought. "She is a tall tower,* without a foundation, that will soon fall down." There was something very lovely and at the same time rather terrible to himself in the state he was now in. Things he said or thought to himself had a kind of poetic power in them. A group of words formed in his mind and the words had power and meaning. He sat playing with the handle of the teacup. Suddenly a great desire to see his own body came over him. He arose and with an apology went out of the room and up a stairway. His wife called to him: "Jane and I are going to drive out into the country. Is there anything I can do for you before we go?"

He stopped on the stairs, but did not answer at once. Her voice was like her face, a little fleshy and heavy. How odd it was for him, a commonplace washing machine manufacturer in a Wisconsin town,* to be thinking in this way, to be noting all these little details of life. He resorted to a trick, wanting to hear his daughter's voice. "Did you call to me, Jane?" he asked. The daughter answered, explaining that it was her mother who had spoken and repeating what had been said. He answered that he wanted nothing but to lie down for an hour and went on up the stairs and into his own room. The daughter's voice, like the mother's, seemed to represent her exactly. It was young and clear, but had no resonance. He closed the door to his room and bolted it. Then he began taking off his clothes.

Now he was not in the least weary. "I'm sure I must be a little insane. A sane person would not note every little thing that goes on as I do to-day," he thought. He sang softly, wanting to hear his own voice, to in a way test it against the voices of his wife and daughter. He hummed over the words of a negro song that had been in his mind earlier in the day,

> "And before I'd be a slave,
>   I'd be buried in my grave,
>   And go home to my father and be saved."

He thought his own voice all right. The words came out of his throat clearly and there was a kind of resonance too. "Had I tried to sing yesterday it would not have sounded like that," he concluded. The voices of his mind were playing about busily. There was a kind of gaiety in him. The thought that had come that morning when he looked into the eyes of Natalie Swartz came running back. His own body, that was now naked, was a house. He went and stood before a mirror and looked at himself. His body was still slender and healthy looking, outside. "I think I know what all this business is I am going through," he concluded. "A kind of house cleaning is going on. My house has been vacant now for twenty years. Dust has settled on the walls and furniture. Now, for some reason I do not understand, the doors and windows have been thrown open. I shall have to scrub the walls and the floors, make everything sweet and clean as it is in Natalie's house. Then I shall invite people in to visit me." He ran his hands over his naked body, over his breasts,* arms, and legs. Something within him was laughing.

He went and threw himself, thus naked on the bed. There were four sleeping rooms in the upper

23

floor of the house. His own was at a corner and there were doors opening into his wife's and his daughter's rooms. When he had first married his wife they had slept together, but when the baby came they gave that up and never did it afterward. Once in a long while now he went in to his wife at night. She wanted him, let him know in some woman's way that she wanted him, and he went, not happily or eagerly, but because he was a man and she a woman and it was done. The thought wearied him a little. "Well it hasn't happened for some weeks." He did not want to think about it.

He owned a horse and carriage that was kept at a livery stable and now it was being driven up to the door of the house. He heard the front door close. His wife and daughter were driving out into the country. The window of his room was open and a breeze blew in and across his body.* The next-door neighbor had a garden and cultivated flowers. The air that came in was fragrant. The sounds were all soft, quiet sounds. Sparrows chirped. A large winged insect flew against the screen that covered the window and crawled slowly toward the top. Away off somewhere the bell of a locomotive began to ring. Perhaps it was on the tracks by his factory where Natalie was now sitting at her desk. He turned to look at the winged thing, crawling slowly. The little voices that lived within one's body were not always serious. Sometimes they played like children. One of the voices declared that the eyes of the insect were looking at him with approval. Now the insect was speaking. "You are a devil of

24

a fellow to have been so long asleep," it said. The bell of the locomotive could still be heard, coming from a long distance, softly. "I'll tell Natalie what that winged fellow had to say," he thought and smiled at the ceiling. His cheeks became flushed and he slept quietly with his hands thrown above his head, as a child sleeps.

III

WHEN he awoke an hour later he was at first
frightened. He looked about the room wondering
if he had been ill.

Then his eyes began an inventory of the furniture of the room. He did not like anything there.
Had he lived for twenty years of his life among
such things? They were no doubt all right. He
knew little of such things. Few men did. A
thought came. How few men in America ever
really thought of the houses they lived in, of the
clothes they wore. Men were willing to go through
a long life without any effort to decorate their bodies, to make lovely and full of meaning the dwellings in which they lived. His own clothes were
hanging on a chair where he had thrown them when
he came into the room. In a moment he would get
up and put them on. Thousands of times, since he
had come to manhood, he had gone through the
performance of clothing his body without thought.
The clothes had been bought casually at some store.
Who had made them? What thought had been
given to the making of them or to the wearing of
them either? He looked at his body lying on the
bed. The clothes would enclose his body, wrap it
about.

26

A thought came into his mind, rang across the spaces of his mind like a bell heard across fields: "Nothing either animate or inanimate* can be beautiful that is not loved."

Getting off the bed he dressed quickly and hurrying out of the room ran down a flight of stairs to the floor below. At the foot of the stairs he stopped. He felt suddenly old and weary and thought perhaps he had better not try to go back to the factory that afternoon. There was no need of his presence there. Everything was going all right. Natalie would attend to anything that came up.

"A fine business if I, a respectable business man with a wife and a grown daughter,*get myself involved in an affair with Natalie Swartz, the daughter of a man who when he was alive ran a low saloon and of that terrible old Irish woman who is the scandal of the town and who when she is drunk talks and yells so that the neighbors* threaten to have her arrested and are only held back because they have sympathy for the daughters.

"The fact is that a man may work and work to make a decent place for himself and then by a foolish act all may be destroyed. I'll have to watch myself a little. I've been working too steadily. Perhaps I'd better take a vacation. I don't want to get into a mess," he thought. How glad he was that, although he had been in a state all day long, he had said nothing to anyone that would betray his condition.

He stood with his hand on the railing of the

27

stairs. At any rate he had been doing a lot of thinking for the last two or three hours. "I haven't been wasting my time."

A notion came. After he married and when he had found out his wife was frightened and driven within herself by every outburst of passion and that as a result there was not much joy in making love to her he had formed a habit of going off on secret expeditions. It had been easy enough to get away. He told his wife he was going on a business trip. Then he went somewhere, to the city of Chicago usually. He did not go to one of the big hotels, but to some obscure place on a side street.

Night came and he set out to find himself a woman. Always he went through the same kind of rather silly performance. He was not given to drinking, but he now took several drinks. One might go at once to some house where women were to be had, but he really wanted something else. He spent hours wandering in the streets.

There was a dream. One vainly hoped to find, wandering about somewhere, a woman who by some miracle would love with freedom and abandon. Along through the streets one went usually in dark badly lighted places where there were factories and warehouses and poor little dwellings. One wanted a golden woman to step up out of the filth of the place in which one*walked. It was insane and silly and one knew these things, but one persisted insanely. Amazing conversations were imagined. Out from the shadow of one of the dark buildings the woman was to step. She was also lonely, hungry, defeated. One went boldly up to her and began at once a conversation filled with strange and beautiful words. Love came flooding their two bodies.

Well perhaps that was exaggerated a little. No doubt one was never quite fool enough to expect anything so wonderful as all that. At any rate what one did was to wander about in the dark streets thus for hours and in the end take up with some prostitute. The two hurried silently off into a little room. Uh. There was always the feeling, "Perhaps*other men have*been in here with her already to-night." There was a halting attempt at conversation. Could they get to know each other, this woman and this man? The woman had a businesslike air. The night was not over and her work was done at night. Too much time must not be wasted. From her point of view a great deal of time had to be wasted in any event. Often one walked half the night without making any money at all.

After such an adventure John Webster came home the next day feeling very mean and unclean. Still he did work better at the office and at night for a long time he slept better. For one thing he kept his mind on affairs and did not give way to dreams and to vague thoughts. When one was running a factory that was an advantage.

Now he stood at the foot of the stairs, thinking perhaps he had better go off on such an adventure again. If he stayed at home and sat all day and every day in the presence of Natalie Swartz there

29

was no telling what would happen. One might as well face facts. After his experience of that morning, his looking into her eyes,*in just the same way he had, the life of the two people in the office would be changed. A new thing would have come into the very air they breathed together. It would be better if he did not go back to the office, but went off at once and took a train to Chicago or Milwaukee. As for his wife—he had got that notion into his head of a kind of death of the flesh. He closed his eyes and leaned against the stair railing. His mind became a blank.

A door leading into the dining room of the house opened and a woman stepped forth. She was the Webster's one servant and had been in the house for many years. Now she was past fifty and as she stood before John Webster he looked at her as he hadn't for a long time. A multitude of thoughts came quickly, like a handful of shot thrown against a window pane.

The woman standing before him was tall and lean and her face was marked by deep lines. It was an odd thing, the notions men had got into their heads about the beauty of women. Perhaps Natalie Swartz, when she was fifty, would look much like this woman.

Her name was Katherine and her coming to work for the Websters long ago had brought on a quarrel between John Webster and his wife. There had been a wreck on the railroad near the Webster factory and this woman was traveling in the day coach of the wrecked train with a man much younger than

herself, who was killed. A young man of Indianapolis, who worked in a bank, had run away with a
woman who was a servant in his father's house and
after he disappeared a large sum of money was
missed at the bank. He had been killed in the
wreck as he sat with the woman and all trace of
him had been lost until someone from Indianapolis,
quite by chance, saw and recognized Katherine on
the streets of her adopted town. The question
asked was, what had become of the money, and
Katherine had been accused of knowing and of con-
cealing it.*

Mrs.*Webster had wanted to discharge her at
once and there had been a quarrel in which the
husband had in the end come out victorious. For
some reason the whole strength of his being had
been put into the matter and one night as he stood
in the common bedroom with his wife he had made
a pronouncement so strong that he himself was surprised by the words that came from his lips. "If
this woman goes out of this house without going
voluntarily then I go also," he had said.

Now John Webster stood in the hallway of his
house looking at the woman who had been the cause
of the quarrel long ago. Well, he had seen her
going silently about the house almost every day
during the long years since that thing happened, but
he had not looked at her as he did now. When
she grew older Natalie Swartz might look as this
woman now looked. If he were to be a fool and
run away with Natalie, as that young fellow from
Indianapolis had once run away with this woman,

31

and if it fell out there was no railroad wreck he might some day be living with a woman who looked somewhat as Katherine now looked.

The thought did not alarm him. It was on the whole rather a sweet thought. "She has lived and sinned and suffered," he thought. There was about the woman's person a kind of strong quiet dignity and it was reflected in her physical being. There was no doubt a kind of dignity coming into his own thoughts too. The notion of going off to Chicago or Milwaukee to walk through dirty streets hungering for the golden woman to come to him out of the filth of life was quite gone now.

The woman Katherine was smiling at him. "I did not eat any lunch because I did not feel like eating but now I'm hungry. Is there anything to eat in the house, anything you might get for me without too much trouble?" he asked.

She lied cheerfully. She had just prepared lunch for herself in the kitchen but now offered it to him.*

He sat at the table eating the food Katherine had prepared. Outside the house the sun was shining. It was only a little after two o'clock and the afternoon and evening were before him. It was strange how the Bible, the older Testaments, kept asserting themselves in his mind. He had never been much of a Bible reader. There was perhaps a kind of massive splendor* to the prose of the book that now fell into step with his own thoughts. In that time, when men lived on the hills and on the plains with their flocks, life lasted in the body of a

32

man or woman a long time. Men were spoken of who had lived for several hundred years. Perhaps there was more than one way to reckon the length of life. In his own case—if he could live every day as fully as he had been living this day, life would be for him lengthened indefinitely.

Katherine came into the room bringing more food and a pot of tea and he looked up and smiled at her. Another thought came. "It would be an amazingly beautiful thing to have happen in the world if everyone, every living man, woman, and child, should suddenly, by a common impulse, come out of their houses, out of the factories and stores, come, let us say, into a great plain, where everyone could see everyone else, and if they should there and then, all of them, in the light of day, with everyone in the world knowing fully what everyone else in the world was doing, if they should all by one common impulse commit the most unforgivable sin of which they were conscious, what a great cleansing time that would be."

His mind made a kind of riot of pictures and he ate the food Katherine had set before him without thought of the physical act of eating. Katherine started to go out of the room and then, noting that he was unaware of her presence, stopped by the door leading into the kitchen and stood looking at him. He had never known that she had been aware of the struggle he had gone through for her many years before. Had he not made that struggle she would not have stayed on in the house. As a matter of fact, on that evening when he had declared that if she were to be made to leave he would leave also, the door to the bedroom upstairs was a little ajar and she was in the hallway downstairs. She had packed her few belongings and had them in a bundle and had intended to steal away somewhere. There was no point to her staying. The man she loved was dead and now she was being hounded by the newspapers and there was a threat that if she did not tell where the money was hidden she would be sent to prison. As for the money—* she did not believe the man who had been killed knew any more about it than she did. No doubt there was money stolen and then, because he had run away with her, the crime was put upon her lover.* The affair was very simple. The young man worked in the bank* and was engaged to be married to a woman of his own class. And then one night he and Katherine were alone in his father's house and something happened between them.

As she stood watching her employer eat the food she had prepared for herself, Katherine thought proudly of an evening long before when she had quite recklessly become the sweetheart of another man. She remembered the fight John Webster had once made for her and thought with contempt of the woman who was her employer's wife.

"That such a man should have such a woman," she thought, recalling the long heavy figure of Mrs. Webster.

As though aware of her thoughts the man again turned and smiled at her. "I am eating the food she had prepared for herself," he told himself, and

34

got quickly up from the table. He went out into the hallway and having taken his hat from a rack lighted a cigarette. Then he returned to the dining room door. The woman stood by the table looking at him and he in turn looked at her. There was no embarrassment. "If I should go away with Natalie and she should become like Katherine* it would be fine," he thought. "Well, well, good bye," he said haltingly and turning walked rapidly out of the house.*

As John Webster walked along the street the sun was shining and as there was a light breeze a few leaves were falling from the maple shade trees with which the streets were lined. Soon there would be frost and the trees would be all afire with color.* If one could only be aware, glorious days were ahead.* Even in the Wisconsin town one might have glorious days. There was a little pang of hunger, a new kind of hunger, within him as he stopped and stood for a moment looking up and down the residence street on which he had been walking. Two hours before, lying naked on the bed in his own house, he had been having the thoughts concerning clothes and houses. It was a charming thought to play with but brought sadness too. Why was it that so many houses along the street were ugly? Were people unaware? Could anyone be quite completely unaware? Could one wear ugly commonplace clothes, live always in an ugly or commonplace house in a commonplace street of a commonplace town and remain always unaware?

35

Now he was thinking of things he decided had better be left out of the thoughts of a business man. However, for this one day, he would give himself over to the thinking of any thought that came into his head. To-morrow* things would be different. He would become again what he had always been (with the exception of a few slips, times when he had been rather as he was now), a quiet orderly man going about his business and not given to foolishness. He would run his washing machine business and try to keep his mind on that. In the evenings he would read the newspapers and keep abreast of the events of the day.

"I don't go on a bat very often. I deserve a little vacation," he thought rather sadly.

Ahead of him in the street, almost two blocks ahead, a man walked. John Webster had met the man once. He was* a professor in a small college of the town, and once, two or three years before, there had been an effort made, on the part of the college president, to raise money among local business men to help the school through a financial crisis. A dinner was given and attended by a number of the college faculty and by an organization called the Chamber of Commerce to which John Webster belonged. The man who now walked before him had been at the dinner and he and the washing machine manufacturer had been seated together. He wondered if he might now presume on that brief acquaintanceship to go and talk with the man. He had been thinking rather unusual thoughts to come into a man's head and perhaps, if he could talk with some other man and in particular with a man whose business in life it was to have thoughts and to understand thought, something might be gained.

There was a narrow strip of grass between the sidewalk and the roadway and along this John Webster began to run. He just grabbed his hat in his hand and ran bareheaded for perhaps two hundred yards and then stopped and looked quietly up and down the street.

It was all right, after all. Apparently no one had seen his strange performance. There were no people sitting on the porches of the houses along the street. He thanked God for that.

Ahead of him the college professor went soberly along with a book under his arm, unaware that he was followed. When he saw that his absurd performance had escaped notice John Webster laughed. "Well, I went to college myself once. I've heard enough college professors talk. I don't know why I should expect anything from one of that stripe."

Perhaps to speak of the things that had been in his mind that day something almost like a new language would be required.

There was that thought about Natalie being a house kept clean and sweet for living, a house into which one might go gladly and joyfully. Could he, a washing machine manufacturer of a Wisconsin town, stop on the street a college professor and say —"I want to know, Mr. College Professor, if your house is clean and sweet for living so that people may come into it and, if it is so, I want you to tell

37

me how you went about it to cleanse*your house."

The notion was absurd. It made one laugh to even think of any such thing. There would have to be new figures of speech, a new way of looking at things. For one thing people would have to be more truly aware of themselves than they had ever been before.

Almost in the centre of town and before a stone building that was some kind of public institution there was a small park with benches and John Webster stopped following the college professor and went and sat on one of them. From where he sat he could see along two of the principal business thoroughfares.

It wasn't a thing done by prosperous washing machine manufacturers, this sitting on benches in the park in the middle of the afternoon but he, at the moment, did not much care. To tell the truth the place for such a man as himself, who owned a factory where many men were employed, was at his desk in his own office. In the evening one might stroll about, read the newspapers or go to the theatre but now, at this hour, the thing was to attend to affairs, be on the job.

He smiled at the thought of himself lolling there on the park bench like a public idler or a tramp. On other benches in the little park sat other men and that was the kind of men they were. Well, they were the kind of fellows who didn't fit into things, who hadn't jobs. One could tell that by looking at them. There was a kind of hang-dog air about them and although two of the men on a nearby bench

38

talked to each other they did it in a dull listless way that showed they were not really interested in what they were saying. Were men, when they talked, ever really interested in what they said to each other?

John Webster put his arms above his head and stretched. He was more aware of himself, of his own body, than he had been for years. "There's something going on like the breaking up of a long hard winter. Spring is coming in me," he thought and the thought pleased him like a caress from the hand of someone he loved.*

Weary tired moments had been coming to him all day long and now another came. He was like a train running through a mountainous country and occasionally passing through tunnels. In one moment the world about him was all alive and then it was just a dull dreary place that frightened him.* The thought that came to him was something like this—"Well, here I am. There is no use denying it, something unusual has happened to me. Yesterday I was one thing. Now I am something else. About me everywhere are these people I have always known, here in this town. Down that street there before me, at the corner there, in that stone building, is the bank where I do the banking business for my factory. It happens that just at this particular time I do not owe them any money, but a year from now I may be in debt to that institution up to my eyebrows. There have been times, in the years I have lived and worked as a manufacturer, when I was altogether in the power of the men who now sit at desks behind

39

those stone walls.   Why they didn't close me up
and take my business away from me I don't know.
Perhaps they did not think it worth while and then,
perhaps, they felt, if they left me on there I would
be working for them anyway.   At any rate now,*it
doesn't seem to matter much what such an institution
as a bank may decide to do.

"One can't quite make out what other men think.
Perhaps they do not think at all.

"If I come right down to it I suppose I've never
done much thinking myself.   Perhaps the whole
business of life, here in this town and everywhere
else, is just a kind of accidental affair.   Things happen.   People are swept along, eh?   That's the way
it must be."

It was incomprehensible to him and his mind soon
grew weary of trying to think further along that
road.

It went back to the matter of people and houses.
Perhaps one could speak of that matter to Natalie.
There was something simple and clear about her.
"She has been working for me for three years now
and it is strange I've never thought much about her
before.   She has a way of keeping things clear and
straight.   Everything has gone better since she has
been with me."

It would be a thing to think about if all the time,
since she had been with him, Natalie had understood the things that were just now becoming a little
plain to him.   Suppose, from the very beginning,
she had been ready to have him go within herself.

One could get quite romantic about the matter if one allowed oneself to think about it.

There she would be, you see, that Natalie. She got out of bed in the morning and while she was there, in her own room, in the little frame house out at the edge of town, she said a little prayer.* Then she walked along the streets and down along the railroad tracks to her work and to sit all day in the presence of a man.

It was an interesting thought, just to suppose, as a kind of playful diversion let us say, that she, that Natalie, was pure and clean.

In that case she wouldn't be thinking much of herself. She loved, that is to say she had opened the doors of herself.

One had a picture of her standing with the doors of her body open. Something constantly went out of her and into the man in whose presence she spent the day. He was unaware, was in fact too much absorbed in his own trivial affairs* to be aware.

Her own self also began to be absorbed with his affairs, to take the load of small and unimportant details of business off his mind in order that he in turn become aware of her, standing thus, with the doors of her body opened. How clean, sweet, and fragrant the house within which she lived!* Before one went within such a house one would have to cleanse oneself too. That was clear. Natalie had done it with prayers and devotion, single-minded devotion to the interests of another. Could one cleanse one's own house that way? Could one be as much the man as Natalie was the woman? It was a test.

As for the matter of houses—if one got thinking of one's*own body in that way where would it all end?* One might go further and think of one's*own body as a town, a city, as the world.

It was a road to madness too. One might think of people constantly passing in and out of each other. In all the world there would be no more secrecy. Something like a great wind would sweep through the world.

"A people drunk with life. A people drunk and joyous with life."

The sentences rang through John Webster like great bells ringing. He sat upright on the park bench. Had the listless fellows sitting about him on other benches heard the words? For just a moment he thought the words might be running like living things through the streets of his town, stopping people on the streets, making people look up from their work in offices and factories.*

"One had better go a little slow and not get oneself*out of hand," he told himself.

He*began trying to think along another road. Across a little stretch of grass and a roadway before him there was a store with trays of fruit, oranges, apples, grapefruit,* and pears arranged on the sidewalk and now a wagon stopped at the store door and began to unload other things. He looked long and hard at the wagon and at the store front.

His mind slipped off at a new tangent. There he was, himself, John Webster, sitting on that bench in a park in the very heart of a town in the state of

Wisconsin. It was fall and nearly time for frost to come, but there was still new life in the grass. How green the grass was in the little park! The trees were alive too. Soon now they would flame with color*and then sleep for a period. To all the world of living green things there would come the flame of evening and then the night of winter.

Out before the world of animal life the fruits of the earth would be poured. Out of the ground they would come, off trees and bushes, out of the seas, lakes, and rivers, the things that were to maintain animal life during the period when the world of vegetable life slept the sweet sleep of winter.

It was a thing to think about too. Everywhere, all about him must be men and women who lived altogether unaware of such things. To tell the truth he had himself been, all his life, unaware. He had just eaten food, stuffed it into his body through his mouth. There had been no joy. He had not really tasted things, smelled things. How filled with fragrant suggestive smells life might be!*

It must have come about that as men and women went out of the fields and hills to live in cities, as factories grew and as the railroads and steamboats came to pass the fruits of the earth back and forth a kind of dreadful unawareness must have grown in people. Not touching things with their hands people lost the sense of them. That was it, perhaps.

John Webster remembered that, when he was a boy, such matters were differently arranged. He lived in the town and knew nothing much of country life, but at that time town and country were more closely wed.

In the fall, at just this time of the year,* farmers used to drive into town and deliver things at his father's house. At that time everyone had great cellars under his house*and in the cellars were bins that were to be filled with potatoes, apples, turnips.* There was a trick man had learned.* Straw was brought in from fields near the town and pumpkins, squashes, heads of cabbage, and*other solid vegetables were wrapped in straw and put into a cool part of the cellar. He remembered that his mother wrapped pears in bits of paper and kept them sweet and fresh for months.

As for himself, although he did not live in the country he was, at that time, aware of something quite tremendous going on. Wagons arrived*at his father's house. On Saturdays a farm woman, who drove an old gray*horse, came to the front door and knocked. She was bringing the Websters their weekly supply of butter and eggs and often a chicken for the Sunday dinner. John Webster's mother went to the door to meet her and the child ran along, clinging to his mother's skirts.

The farm woman came into the house and sat up stiffly in a chair in the parlor*while her basket was being emptied and while the butter was being taken out of its stone jar. The boy stood with his back to the wall in a corner and studied her. Nothing was said. What strange hands she had, so unlike his mother's hands, that were soft and white. The farm woman's hands were brown and the knuckles

44

were like the bark-covered knobs that sometimes grew on the trunks of trees. They were hands to take hold of things, to take hold of things firmly.

After the men from the country had come and had put the things in the bins in the cellar it was fine to go down there in the afternoon when one had come home from school. Outside the leaves were all coming off the trees and everything looked bare. One felt a little sad and almost frightened at times and the visits to the cellar were reassuring. The rich smell of things, fragrant and strong smells! One got an apple out of one of the bins and stood eating it. In a far corner there were the dark bins where the pumpkins and squashes were buried in straw and everywhere, along the walls, were the glass jars of fruit his mother had put up. How many of them, what a plenitude of everything. One could eat and eat and still there would be plenty.

At night sometimes, when one had gone upstairs and had got*into bed, one thought of the cellar and of the farm woman and the farm men.* Outside the house it was dark and a wind was blowing. Soon there would be winter and snow and skating. The farm woman with the strange, strong-looking hands had driven the gray* horse* off along the street on which the Webster house stood, and around a corner. One had stood at a window down stairs and had watched her out of sight. She had gone off into some mysterious place, spoken of as the country. How big was the country and how far away was it? Had she got there yet? It was night now and very dark. The wind was blowing. Was she still driving

45

the gray*horse on and on, the reins held in her strong brown hands?

The boy had got into bed and had pulled the covers up about him. His mother came into the room and after kissing him went away taking his lamp. He was safe in the house. Near him, in another room, his father and mother slept. Only the country woman, with the strong hands, was now out there alone in the night. She was driving the gray*horse on and on into the darkness, into the strange place from which came all the good, rich-smelling things, now stored*away in the cellar under the house.*

IV

"WELL, hello you, Mr. Webster. This is a fine place for you to be day-dreaming. I've been standing here and looking at you for several minutes and you haven't even seen me."

John Webster jumped to his feet. The afternoon was passing and already there was a kind of grayness*falling over the trees and the grass in the little park. The late afternoon sun was shining on the figure of the man who stood before him and, although the man was short of stature and slight, his shadow on the stone walk was grotesquely long. The man was evidently amused at the thought of the prosperous manufacturer day-dreaming there in the park and laughed softly,* his body swaying a little back and forth. The shadow also swayed. It was like a thing hung on a pendulum, swinging back and forth, and even as John Webster sprang to his feet a sentence went through his mind. "He takes life with a long slow easy swing. How does that happen? He takes life with a long slow easy swing," his mind said. It seemed like a fragment of a thought snatched out of nowhere, a fragmentary dancing little thought.

The man who stood before him owned a small second-hand book store on a side street along which John Webster was in the habit of walking as he went

47

back and forth to his factory.   On summer evenings the man sat in a chair before his shop and made comments on the weather and on passing events to the people going up and down the sidewalk.   Once when John Webster was with his banker, a gray dignified looking man, he had been somewhat embarrassed because the bookseller called out his name. He had never done it until that day and never did it afterward.   The manufacturer had become self-conscious and had explained the matter to the banker.*   "I really don't know the man.   I was never in his shop," he said.

In the park John Webster stood before the little man deeply embarrassed.   He told a harmless lie. "I've had a headache all day and sat down here for a moment," he said sheepishly.   It was annoying that he felt like apologizing.   The little man smiled knowingly.   "You ought to take something for that. It might get a man like you into a hell of a mess," he said and walked away, his long shadow dancing behind him.

With a shrug of his shoulders John Webster went rapidly through a crowded business street.   He was quite sure now that he knew what he wanted to do. He did not loiter and give way to vague thoughts, but walked briskly along the street.   "I'll keep my mind occupied," he decided.   "I'll think about my business and how to develop it."   During the week before, an advertising man from Chicago had come into his office and had talked to him about advertising his washing machine in the big national magazines. It would cost a good deal of money, but the advertising man had said that he could raise his selling price and sell many more machines. That sounded possible. It would make the business a big one, an institution of national prominence, and himself a big figure in the industrial world. Other men had got into a position like that through the power of advertising.* Why shouldn't he do something of the sort?*

He tried to think about the matter, but his mind didn't work very well. It was a blank. What happened was that he walked along with his shoulders thrown back and felt childishly important about nothing. He had to be careful or he would begin laughing at himself. There was within him a lurking fear that in a few minutes he would begin laughing at the figure of John Webster as a man of national importance in the industrial world and the fear made him hurry faster than ever. When he got to the railroad tracks that ran down to his factory he was almost running. It was amazing.* The advertising man from Chicago could use big words, apparently without being in any danger of suddenly beginning to laugh. When John Webster was a young fellow and had just come out of college, that was when he read a great many books and sometimes thought he would like to become a writer of books, at that time he had often thought he wasn't cut out to be a business man at all. Perhaps he was right. A man who hadn't any more sense than to laugh at himself had better not try to become a figure of national importance in the industrial world, that was sure. It wanted serious fellows to carry off such positions successfully.

Well now he had begun to be a little sorry for himself, that he was not cut out to be a big figure in the industrial world. What a childish fellow he was. He began to scold himself, "Won't I ever grow up?"*

As he hurried along the railroad tracks, trying to think, trying not to think, he kept his eyes turned to the ground and something attracted his attention. To the west, over the tops of distant trees and across the shallow river beside which his factory stood, the sun was just going down and its rays were suddenly caught by something that looked like a piece of glass lying among the stones on the railroad roadbed.

He stopped his rush along the tracks and leaned over to pick it up. It was something, perhaps a jewel of some sort, perhaps just a cheap little plaything some child had lost. The stone was about the size and shape of a small bean and was dark green. When the rays of the sun fell on it, as he held it in his hand, the color changed. After all it might be a valuable thing. "Perhaps some woman, riding on a train through the town, has lost it out of her ring or out of a brooch she wears at her throat," he thought and had a momentary picture floating in his mind. In the picture there was a tall strong fair woman, standing, not on a train but on a hill above a river. The river was wide and as it was winter was covered with ice. The woman

50

had one hand raised and was pointing. A ring was on her finger and the small green stone was set in the ring. He could see everything very minutely. The woman stood on the hill and the sun shone on her and the stone in the ring was now pale, now dark like the waters of a sea, and beside the woman stood a man, a rather heavy-looking man with gray hair, with whom the woman was in love. The woman was saying something to the man about the stone set in the ring and John Webster could hear the words very distinctly. What strange words she was saying. "My father gave it to me and told me to wear it for all my loves. He called it, 'the jewel of life,' " she said.*

Hearing the rumble of a train, far away somewhere in the distance, John Webster got off the tracks. There was at just that place a high embankment beside the river along which he could walk. "I don't intend to come near being killed by a train as I was this morning when that young negro saved me," he thought. He looked away to the west and to the evening sun and then down at the bed of the river. Now the river was low and only a narrow channel of water ran through wide banks of caked mud.* He put the little green stone in his vest pocket.

"I know what I am going to do," he told himself resolutely. Quickly a plan formed itself in his mind. He would go to his office and hurry through any letters that had come in. Then, without looking at Natalie Swartz, he would get up and go away. There was a train for Chicago at eight o'clock and he would tell his wife he had business in the city and would take the train. What a man had to do in life was to face facts and then act. He would go to Chicago and find himself a woman. When it came right down to the truth he would go on a regular bat. He would find himself a woman and he would get drunk and if he felt like doing it would stay drunk for several days.

There were times when it was perhaps necessary to be a down-right*rotter. He would do that too. While he was in Chicago and with the woman he had found he would write a letter to his bookkeeper at the factory and tell him to discharge Natalie Swartz. Then he would write Natalie a letter and send her a large check. He would send her six months' pay. The whole thing might cost him a pretty sum, but anything was better than this going on as he was, a regular crazy kind of man.

As for the woman in Chicago, he would find her all right. One got bold after a few drinks and when one had the money to spend women were always to be had.*

It was too bad that it was so but the truth was that the need of women was a part of a man's make-up and the fact might as well be faced. "When you come down to that, I am a business man and it is a business man's place in the scheme of things to face facts," he decided and suddenly he felt very resolute and strong.

As for Natalie, to tell the truth, there was in her perhaps something that it was a little hard for him to resist. "If there were only my wife it would

52

be different but there is my daughter Jane.   She is a pure young innocent thing and must be protected. I can't let her in for a mess," he told himself as he walked boldly along the little spur of the tracks that led to the door of his factory.*

V

WHEN he had opened the door that led into the little room where he had been sitting and working beside Natalie for three years, he quickly closed it behind him and stood with his back to the door and with his hand on the door-knob, as though for support. Natalie's desk was beside a window at a corner of the room and beyond his own desk and through the window one could see into an empty space beside the spur of tracks that belonged to the railroad company, but in which he had been given the privilege of piling a reserve supply of lumber. The lumber was so piled that, in the soft evening light, the yellow boards made a kind of background for Natalie's figure.

The sun was shining on the lumber pile, the last soft rays of the evening sun. Above the lumber pile there was a space of clear light and into this Natalie's head was thrust.

An amazing and lovely thing had happened.* When the fact of it came into his consciousness something within John Webster was torn open. What a simple thing Natalie had done and yet how significant. He stood with the door-knob grasped in his hand, clinging to the door-knob, and within himself the thing happened he had been trying to avoid.

54

Tears came into his eyes. In all his after life he never lost the sense of that moment. In one instant all within himself was muddy and dirty with the thoughts he had been having about the proposed trip to Chicago and then the mud and dirt was all, as by a quick miracle, swept away.*

"At any other time what Natalie had done might have passed unnoticed," he told himself later, but that fact did not in any way destroy its significance. All of the women who worked in his office as well as the bookkeeper and the men in the factory were in the habit of carrying their lunches and Natalie had brought her lunch on that morning as always. He remembered having seen her come in with it wrapped in a paper package.*

Her home was a long distance away, at the edge of the town. None of the other of his employees came from so great a distance.

And on that noon she had not eaten her lunch. There it was done up in its package and lying on a shelf back of her head.

What had happened was this—at the noon time she had hurried out of the office and had run all the way home to her mother's house. There was no bathtub there, but she had drawn water from a well and put it in a common washtub in a shed back of the house. Then she had plunged into the water and washed her body from head to foot.

After she had done that she had gone upstairs and arrayed herself in a special dress, the best one she owned, the one she had always kept for Sunday after-noons and for special occasions. As she dressed, her old mother, who had been following her about, swearing at her and demanding an explanation, stood at the foot of the stairway leading to her room and called her vile names. "You little whore, you are planning to go out with some man to-night so you are fixing yourself up as though you were about to be married. A swell chance either of my two daughters have got to ever get themselves husbands. If you've got any money in your pocket you give it to me. I wouldn't care so much about your traipsing around if you ever got any money," she declared in a loud voice. On the evening before she had got money from one of the daughters and during the morning had provided herself with a bottle of whiskey.* Now she was enjoying herself.

Natalie had paid no attention to her. When she was fully dressed she hurried down the stairs, brushing the old woman aside, and half ran back to the factory. The other women employed there had laughed when they saw her coming. "What's Natalie up to?"*they had asked each other.

John Webster stood looking at her and thinking. He knew all about what she had done and why she had done it although he had seen nothing. Now she did not look at him, but, turning her head slightly, looked out over the lumber piles.

Well then she had known all day what had been going on within himself.* She had understood his sudden desire to come within herself so she had run home to bathe and array herself. "It was like washing the door sills of her house and hanging

56

newly laundered curtains at the windows," he thought whimsically.

"You have changed your dress, Natalie," he said aloud. It was the first time he had ever called her by that name. Tears were in his eyes and his knees suddenly felt weak. He walked, a little unsteadily, across the room, and knelt beside her. Then he put his head in her lap and felt her broad strong hand in his hair and on his cheek.

For a long time he knelt thus breathing deeply. The thoughts*of the morning came back. After all though he wasn't thinking. The things going on within him were not so definite as thoughts. If his body were a house it was now the cleansing time for that house. A thousand little creatures were running through the house, going swiftly up and down stairs, opening windows, laughing, crying to each other.* The rooms of his house echoed with new sounds, with joyous sounds. His body trembled. Now, after this had happened, a new life would begin for him. His body would be more alive. He would see things, smell things, taste things, as never before.

He looked up into Natalie's face. How much did she know of all this? Well, she would no doubt be unable to say it in words but there was a way in which she did understand. She had run home to bathe and array herself. That was the reason he knew she knew. "How long have you been ready for this to happen?" he asked.

"For a year," she said. She had grown a little

pale. In the room it was beginning to grow dark.

She got up and putting him gently aside went to the door leading into the outer office and slipped a bolt that would prevent the door being opened.

Now she was standing with her back to the door and with her hand on the knob as he had been standing some time before. He got up and went to his own desk, near a window that faced the spur of the railroad track, and sat in his office chair. Leaning forward he buried his face in his two arms. The trembling, shaking thing continued to go on within him. Still the little joyous voices called. The cleansing within*was going on and on.

Natalie spoke of the affairs of the office. "There were some letters, but I answered them and even dared to sign your name. I did not want you to be bothered to-day."

She came to where he sat, leaning forward on the desk, trembling, and knelt beside him. After a time he put an arm about her shoulder.

The outside noises of the office went steadily on. In the outer office someone was running a typewriting machine. It was quite dark in the inner office now, but above the railroad track, some two or three hundred yards away, there was a lamp*suspended in the air and when it was lighted a faint light came into the dark room and fell upon the two crouched figures. Presently a whistle blew and the workers from the factory went off up the spur of track. In the outer office the four people were getting ready to go home.

In a few minutes they came out, closing a door behind them, and walked also along the spur of track. Unlike the workers from the factory they knew the two people were still in the inner office and were curious. One of the three women came boldly up to the window and looked in.

She went back to the others and they stood for a few minutes, making a small intense group in the half darkness.* Then they went slowly away.

When the group broke up, on the embankment above the river, the bookkeeper, a man of thirty-five, and the oldest of the three women went to the right along the tracks while the other two went to the left.* The bookkeeper and the woman he walked with did not speak of what had been seen.* They walked for several hundred yards together and then parted, turning from the tracks into separate streets. When the bookkeeper was alone he began to worry about the future. "You'll see. Within a few months I'll have to be looking for a new place. When that sort of thing begins business goes to pieces." * He was worried about the fact that, as he had a wife and two children and did not get a very large salary, he had no money saved. "Damn that Natalie Swartz. I'll bet she's a whore, that's what I'll bet," he muttered as he went along.

As for the two remaining women, one of them wanted to speak of the two people kneeling together in the dark office while the other did not. There were several ineffectual attempts at talk of the matter on the part of the older of the two and then they also parted. The youngest of the three,*the one who had smiled at John Webster that morning

59

when he had just come out of Natalie's presence and when he had for the first time realized that the doors of her being were open to him, went along the street past the door of the bookseller's shop and up a climbing street into the lighted business section of the town. She kept smiling as she went along and it was because of something she herself did not understand.

It was because she was herself one in whom the little voices talked and now they were going busily. Some phrase, picked up somewhere, from the Bible perhaps when she was a young girl and went to Sunday school, or from some book, kept saying itself over and over in her mind. What a charming combination of plain words in everyday use among people. She kept saying them in her mind and after a time, when she came to a place in the street where there was no one near, she said them aloud. "And as it turned out there was a marriage in our house," were the words she said.

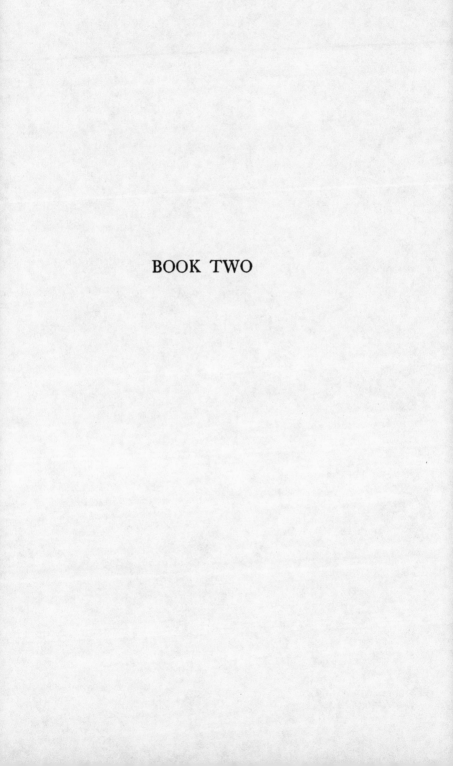

BOOK TWO

I

'As you will remember, the room in which John Webster slept was at a corner of the house, upstairs. From one of his two windows he looked out into the garden of a German who owned a store in his town but whose real interest in life was the garden. All through the year he worked at it and had John Webster been more alive, during the years he lived in the room, he might have got keen pleasure out of looking down upon his neighbor*at work. In the early morning and late afternoon the German*was always to be seen, smoking his pipe and digging, and a great variety of smells came floating up and in at the window of the room above, the sour acid smell of vegetables decaying, the rich heady smell of stable manure and then, all through the summer and late into the fall, the fragrant smell of roses and the marching procession of the flowers of the seasons.

John Webster had lived in his room for many years without much thought of what a room, within which a man lives and the walls of which enclose him like a garment when he sleeps, might be like. It was a square room with one window looking down into the German's garden and another window that faced the blank walls of the German's house. There were three doors—one leading into a hallway, one into the room where his wife slept, and a third that led into his daughter's room.*

One came into the place at night and closed the doors and prepared oneself for sleep. Behind the two walls were the two other people, also preparing for sleep, and behind the walls of the German's house no doubt the same thing was going on. The German had two daughters and a son. They would be going to bed or were already in bed. There was, at that street end, something like a little village of people going to bed or already in bed.

For a good many years John Webster and his wife had not been very intimate. Long ago, when he had found himself married to her he had found also that she had a theory of life, picked up somewhere, perhaps from her parents, perhaps just absorbed out of the general atmosphere of fear in which so many modern women live and breathe, clutched at, as it were, and used as a weapon against too close contact with another. She thought, or believed she thought, that even in marriage a man and woman should not be lovers*except for the purpose of bringing children into the world. The belief threw a sort of heavy air of responsibility about the matter of love-making. One does not go very freely in and out of the body of another when the going in and out involves such heavy responsibility. The doors of the body become rusty and creak. "Well, you see," John Webster, in later years, sometimes explained, "one is quite seriously at the business of bringing another human into the world. Here is the Puritan in full flower. The night has

64

come. From the gardens back of men's houses comes the scent of flowers. Little hushed noises arise followed by silences. The flowers in their gardens have known an ecstasy*unfettered by any awareness of responsibility, but man is something else. For ages he has been taking himself with extraordinary seriousness. The race, you see, must be perpetuated. It must be improved. There is in this affair something of obligation to God and to one's fellow men.* Even when, after long preparation, talk, prayer, and the acquiring of a little wisdom, a kind of abandon is acquired, as one would acquire a new language, one has still achieved something quite foreign to the flowers, the trees, and the life and the carrying on of life among what is called the lower animals."

As for the earnest God-fearing people, among whom John Webster and his wife then lived and as one of whom they had for so many years counted themselves, the chances are no such thing as ecstasy is ever acquired at all. There is instead, for the most part, a kind of cold sensuality tempered by an itching conscience. That life can perpetuate itself at all in such an atmosphere is one of the wonders of the world and proves, as nothing else could, the cold determination of nature not to be defeated.

And so for years the man had been in the habit of coming into his bedroom at night, taking off his clothes, and hanging them on a chair or in a closet and then crawling into bed to sleep heavily. Sleeping was a part of the necessary business of living and if, before he slept, he thought at all he thought of

65

his washing machine business. There was a note due and payable at the bank on the next day and he had no money with which to pay it. He thought of that and of what he could and would say to the banker to induce him to renew the note. Then he thought about the trouble he was having with the foreman at his factory. The man wanted a larger wage and he was trying to think whether or not, if he did not give it to him, the man would quit and put him to the trouble of finding another foreman.

When he slept he did not sleep lightly and no fancies visited his dreams. What should have been a sweet time of renewal became a heavy time filled with distorted dreams.

And then, after the doors of Natalie's body had been swung open for him, he became aware. After that evening when they had knelt together in the darkness it was hard for him to go home in the evening and sit at table with his wife and daughter. "Well, I can't do it," he told himself and ate his evening meal at a restaurant down town. He stayed about, walking in unfrequented streets, talking or in silence beside Natalie and then went with her to her own house, far out at the edge of town. People saw them walking thus together and, as there was no effort at concealment, there was a blaze of talk in the town.

When John Webster went home to his own house his wife and daughter had already gone to bed. "I am very busy at the shop. Do not expect to see much of me for a time," he had said to his wife on the morning after he had told Natalie of his love.

66

He did not intend to stay on in the washing machine business or to continue his married life. What he would do he did not*quite know. He would live with Natalie for one thing. The time had come to do that.

He had spoken of it to Natalie on that first evening of their intimacy. On that evening, after the others were all gone they went to walk together. As they went through the streets people in the houses were sitting down to the evening meal, but the man and woman did not think of eating.*

John Webster's tongue had become loosened and he did a great deal of talking to which Natalie listened in silence. Of the people of the town those he did not know all became romantic figures in his awaking mind.* His fancy wanted to play about them and he let it. They went along a residence street toward the open country beyond and he kept speaking of the people in the houses. "Now Natalie, my woman, you see all these houses here," he said waving his arms to right and left, "well, what do you and I know about what goes on back of these walls?" He kept taking deep breaths as he went along, just as he had done back there at the office when he had run across the room to kneel at Natalie's feet. The little voices within him were still talking. He had been something like this sometimes when he was a boy, but no one had ever understood the riotous play of his fancy and in time he had come to think that letting his fancy go was all foolishness.*
Then when he was a young man and had married there had come a sharp new flare-up*of the fanciful

67

life, but then it had been frozen in him by the fear and the vulgarity that is born of fears. Now it was playing madly. "Now you see, Natalie," he cried, stopping on the sidewalk to take hold of her two hands and swinging them madly back and forth, "now you see, here's how it is. These houses along here look like just ordinary houses, such as you and I live in, but they aren't like that at all. The outer walls are, you see, just things stuck up, like scenery on a stage. A breath can blow the walls down or an outburst of flames can consume them all in an hour. I'll bet you what—I'll bet that what you think is that the people back of the walls of these houses are just ordinary people. They aren't at all. You're all wrong about that, Natalie, my love. The women in the rooms back of these walls are all fair sweet women and you should just go into the rooms. They are hung with beautiful pictures and tapestry and the women have jewels on their hands and in their hair.*

"And so the men and women live together in their houses and there are no good people, only beautiful ones, and children are born and their fancies are allowed to riot all over the place, and no one takes himself too seriously and thinks the whole outcome of human life depends upon himself, and people go out of these houses to work in the morning and come back at night and where they get all the rich comforts of life they have I can't make out. It's because there is really such a rich abundance of everything in the world somewhere and they have found out about it, I suppose."

On their first evening together he and Natalie had walked beyond the town and had got into a country road. They went along this for a mile and then turned into a little side road. There was a great tree growing beside the road and they went to lean against it, standing side by side in silence.

It was after they had kissed that he told Natalie of his plans. "There are three or four thousand dollars in the bank and the factory is worth thirty or forty thousand more. I don't know how much it is worth, perhaps nothing at all.

"At any rate I'll take a thousand dollars and go away with you. I suppose I'll leave some kind of papers making over the ownership of the place to my wife and daughter. That would, I suppose, be the thing to do.

"Then I'll have to talk to my daughter, make her understand what I'm doing and why. Well, I hardly know whether it is possible to make her understand, but I'll have to try. I'll have to try to say something that will stay in her mind so that she in her turn may learn to live and not close and lock the doors of her being as my own doors have been locked. It may take, you see, two or three weeks to think out what I have to say and how to say it. My daughter Jane knows nothing. She is an American middle-class girl and I have helped to make her that. She is a virgin and that, I am afraid, Natalie, you do not understand. The gods have robbed you of your virginity or perhaps it was your old mother, drunk and calling you names, eh? That might have been

69

a help to you. You wanted so much to have some sweet clean thing happen to you, to something deep down in you, that you went about with the doors of your being opened, eh? They did not have to be torn open. Virginity and respectability had not fastened them with bolts and locks. Your mother must quite have killed all notion of respectability in your family, eh Natalie? It is the most wonderful thing in the world to love you and to know that there is something in you that would make the notion of being cheap and second-class impossible to your lover. O, my Natalie, you are a woman strong to be loved."

Natalie did not answer, perhaps did not understand this outpouring of words from him, and John Webster stopped talking and moved about so that he stood directly facing her. They were of about the same height and when he had come close they looked directly into each other's faces. He put up his hands so that they lay on her cheeks and for a long time they stood thus, without words, looking at each other as though they could neither of them get enough of the sight of the face of the other. A late moon came up presently and they moved instinctively out from under the shadow of the tree and went into a field. They kept moving slowly along, stopping constantly and standing thus, with his hands on her cheeks. Her body began to tremble and the tears ran from her eyes. Then he laid her down upon the grass. It was an experience with a woman new in his life. After their first love-making and when their passions were spent she seemed more beautiful to him than before.

He stood within the door of his own house and it was late at night. One did not breathe any too well within those walls. He had a desire to creep through the house, to be unheard, and was thankful when he had got to his own room and had undressed and got into bed without being spoken to.

In bed he lay with eyes open listening to the night noises from without the house. They were not very plain. He had forgotten to open the window. When he had done that a low humming sound arose. The first frost had not come yet and the night was warm. In the garden owned by the German, in the grass in his own back-yard, in the branches of the trees along the streets and far off in the country there was life abundant.

Perhaps Natalie would have a child. It did not matter. They would go away together, live together in some distant place. Now Natalie must be at home in her mother's house and she would also be lying awake. She would be taking deep breaths of the night air. He did that himself.

One could think of her and could also think of the people closer about. There was the German who lived next door. By turning his head he could see faintly the walls of the German's house. His neighbor had a wife, a son and two daughters. Perhaps now they were all asleep. In fancy he went into his neighbor's house, went softly from room to room through the house. There was the old man sleeping beside his wife and in another room the son who had drawn up his legs so that he lay in a little ball. He was a pale slender young man. "Perhaps he has indigestion," whispered John Webster's fancy. In another room the two daughters lay in two beds set closely together. One could just pass between them. They had been whispering to each other before they slept, perhaps of the lover they hoped would come, some time in the future. He stood so close to them that he could have touched their cheeks with his out-stretched fingers. He wondered why it had happened that he had become Natalie's lover instead of the lover of one of these girls. "That could have happened. I could have loved either of them had she opened the doors of herself as Natalie has done."

Loving Natalie did not preclude the possibility of his loving another, perhaps many others. "A rich man might have many marriages," he thought. It was certain that the possibility of human relationship had not even been tapped yet. Something had stood in the way of a sufficiently broad acceptance of life. One had to accept oneself*and the others before one could love.

As for himself he had to accept now his wife and daughter, draw close to them for a little before he went away with Natalie. It was a difficult thing to think about. He lay with wide-open eyes in his bed and tried to send his fancy into his wife's room. He could not do it. His fancy could go into his daughter's room and look at her lying asleep in her bed, but with his wife it was different. Something within him drew back. "Not now. Do not try it. It is not permitted. If she is ever to have a lover now it must be another," a voice within him said.

"Did she do something that has destroyed the possibility of that or did I?" he asked himself sitting up in bed. There was no doubt a human relationship had been spoiled—messed. "It is not permitted. It is not permitted to make a mess on the floor of the temple," the answering voice within said sternly.

To John Webster it seemed that the voices in the room spoke so loudly that as he lay down again and tried to sleep he was a little surprised that they had not awakened from their sleep the others in the house.

II

INTO the air of the Webster house and into the
air also of John Webster's office and factory a new
element had come. On all sides of him there was
a straining at something within. When he was not
alone or in the company of Natalie he no longer
breathed freely. "You have done us an injury.
You are doing us an injury," everyone else seemed
to be saying.

He wondered about that, tried to think about
it. The presence of Natalie gave him each day a
breathing time. When he sat beside her in the
office he breathed freely, the tight thing within him
relaxed. It was because she was simple and
straightforward. She said little, but her eyes spoke
often. "It's all right. I love you. I am not
afraid to love you," her eyes said.

However he thought constantly of the others.
The bookkeeper refused to look into his eyes or
spoke with a new and elaborate politeness. He had
already got into the habit of discussing the matter
of John Webster and Natalie's affair every evening
with his wife. In the presence of his employer he
now felt self-conscious and it was the same with
the two older women in the office.* As he passed

74

through the office the younger of the three* still sometimes looked up and smiled at him.

It was no doubt a fact that no man could do a quite isolated thing in the modern world of men. Sometimes when John Webster was walking homeward late at night, after having spent some hours with Natalie, he stopped and looked about him. The street was deserted and the lights had been put out in many of the houses. He raised his two arms and looked at them. They had recently held a woman, tightly, tightly, and the woman was not the one with whom he had lived for so many years, but a new woman he had found. His arms had held her tightly and her arms had held him. There had been joy in that. Joy had run through their two bodies during the long embrace. They had breathed deeply. Had the breath blown out of their lungs poisoned the air others had to breathe? As to the woman, who was called his wife—she had wanted no such embraces, or, had she wanted them, had been unable to take or give. A notion came to him. "If you love in a loveless world you face others with the sin of not loving," he thought.

The streets lined with houses in which people lived were dark. It was past eleven o'clock, but there was no need to hurry home. When he got into bed he could not sleep. "It would be better just to walk about for an hour yet," he decided and when he came to the corner that led into his own street did not turn, but kept on, going far out to the edge of town and back. His feet made a sharp sound on the stone sidewalks. Sometimes he met

75

a man homeward bound and as they passed the man looked at him with surprise and something like distrust in his eyes. He walked past and then turned to look back. "What are you doing abroad? Why aren't you at home and in bed with your wife?" the man seemed to be asking.

What was the man really thinking? Was there much thinking going on in all the dark houses along the street or did people simply go into them to eat and sleep as he had always gone into his own house? In fancy he got a quick vision of many people lying in beds stuck high in the air. The walls of the houses had receded from them.*

Once, during the year before, there had been a fire in a house on his own street and the front wall of the house had fallen down.* When the fire was put out one walked past in the street and there, laid bare to the public gaze, were two upstairs rooms in which people had lived for many years. Everything was a little burned and charred, but quite intact. In each room there were a bed, one or two chairs, a square piece of furniture with drawers in which shirts or*dresses could be kept, and at the side of the room a closet for other clothes.

The house had quite burned out below and the stairway had been destroyed. When the fire broke out the people must have fled from the rooms like frightened and disturbed insects. One of the rooms had been occupied by a man and woman. There was a dress lying on the floor and a pair of half-burned trousers flung over the back of a chair, while in the second room, evidently occupied by a woman,

76

there were no signs of male attire. The place had made John Webster think of his own married life. "It is as it might have been with us had my wife and I not quit sleeping together. That might have been our room with the room of our daughter Jane beside it," he had thought on the morning after the fire as he walked past and stopped with other curious idlers to gaze up at the scene above.

And now, as he walked alone in the sleeping streets of his town his imagination succeeded in stripping all the walls from all the houses and he walked as in some strange city of the dead. That his imagination could so flame up, running along whole streets of houses and wiping out walls as a wind shakes the branches of the trees, was a new and living wonder to himself. "A life-giving thing has been given to me. For many years I have been dead and now I am alive," he thought. To give the fuller play to his fancy he got off the sidewalk and walked in the centre of the street. The houses lay before him all silent and the late moon had appeared and made black pools under the trees. The houses stripped of their walls were on either side of him.

In the houses the people were sleeping in their beds. How many bodies lying and sleeping close together, babes asleep in cribs, young boys sleeping sometimes two or three in a single bed, young women asleep with their hair fallen down about their faces.

As they slept they dreamed. Of what did they dream? He had a great desire that what had happened to himself and Natalie should happen to all of them. The love-making in the field had after all been but a symbol of something more filled with meaning than the mere act of two bodies embracing, the passage of the seeds of life from one body to another.

A great hope flared up in him. "A time will come when love like a sheet*of fire will run through the towns and cities. It will tear walls away. It will destroy ugly houses. It will tear ugly clothes off the bodies of men and women. They will build anew and build beautifully," he declared aloud. As he walked and talked thus he felt suddenly like a young prophet come out of some far strange clean land to visit with the blessing of his presence the people of the street. He stopped and putting his hands to his head laughed loudly at the picture he had made of himself. "You would think I was another John the Baptist who has been living in a wilderness on locusts and wild honey instead of a washing machine manufacturer in a Wisconsin town," he thought. A window to one of the houses was opened and he heard low voices talking. "Well, I'd better be going home before they lock me up for a crazy man," he thought, getting out of the road and turning out of the street at a nearby corner.*

At the office, during the day, there were no such periods of exhilaration. There only Natalie seemed quite in control of the situation. "She has stout legs and strong feet. She knows how to stand her

78

ground," John Webster thought as he sat at his desk and looked across at her sitting at her desk.

She was not insensible to what was going on about her. Sometimes when he looked suddenly up at her and when she did not know he was looking he saw something that convinced him her hours alone were not now very happy.* There was a tightening about the eyes. No doubt she had her own little hell to face.

Still she went about her work every day outwardly unperturbed. "That old Irish woman, with her temper, her drinking, and her love of loud picturesque profanity has managed to put her daughter through a course of sprouts,"*he decided. It was well Natalie was so level-headed. "The Lord knows she and I may need all of her level-headedness before we are through with our lives," he decided. There was something in women, a kind of power, few men understood. They could stand the gaff. Now Natalie did his work and her own too. When a letter came*she answered it and when there was something to be decided she made the decision. Sometimes she looked across at him as though to say, "Your job, the clearing up you will still have to do in your own house, will be more difficult than anything I shall*have to face. You let me attend to these minor details of our life now. To do that makes the time of waiting less difficult for me."

She did not say anything of the sort in words, being one not given to words, but there was always something in her eyes that made him understand what she wanted to say.

79

After that first love-making in the field they were not lovers again while they remained in the Wisconsin town although every evening they went to walk together. After dining at her mother's house where she had to pass under the questioning eyes of her sister the school teacher, also a silent woman, and to withstand a fiery outbreak from her mother who came to the door to shout questions after her down the street, Natalie came back along the railroad tracks to find John Webster waiting for her in the darkness by the office door. Then they walked boldly through the streets and went into the country and, when they had got upon a country road, went hand in hand, for the most part in silence.

And from day to day, in the office and in the Webster household the feeling of tenseness grew more and more pronounced.

In the house, when he had come in late at night and had crept up to his room, he had a sense of the fact that both his wife and daughter were lying awake, thinking of him, wondering about him, wondering what strange thing had happened to make him suddenly a new man. From what he had seen in their eyes in the day-time he knew that they had both became suddenly aware of him. Now he was no longer the mere bread-winner, the man who goes in and out of his house as a work horse goes in and out of a stable. Now, as he lay in his bed and behind the two walls of his room and the two closed doors, voices were awakening within them, little fearful voices. His mind had got into the habit of thinking of walls and doors. "Some night the walls will fall down and the two doors will open. I must be ready for the time when that happens," he thought.

His wife was one who, when she was excited, resentful, or angry, sank herself into an ocean of silence. Perhaps the whole town knew of his walking about in the evening with Natalie Swartz. Had news of it come to his wife she would not have spoken of the matter to her daughter. There would be just a dense kind of silence in the house and the daughter would know there was something the matter. There had been such times before. The daughter would have become frightened, perhaps it would be just at bottom the fear of change, that something was about to happen that would disturb the steady even passage of days.

One noon, during the second week after the love-making with Natalie, he walked toward the centre of town, intending to go into a restaurant and eat lunch, but instead walked straight ahead down the tracks for nearly a mile. Then, not knowing exactly what impulse had led him, he went back to the office. Natalie and all the others except the youngest of the three women had gone out.* Perhaps the air of the place had become so heavy with unexpressed thoughts and feelings that none of them wanted to stay there when they were not working.* The day was bright and warm, a golden and red Wisconsin day of early October.

He walked into the inner office, stood a moment looking vaguely about and then came out again.

The young woman sitting there arose. Was she going to say something to him about the affair with Natalie? He also stopped and stood looking at her. She was a small woman with a sweet womanly mouth, gray*eyes, and with a kind of tiredness expressing itself in her whole being. What did she want? Did she want him to go ahead with the love affair with Natalie, of which she no doubt knew, or did she want him to stop? "It would be dreadful if she should try to speak about it," he thought and then at once, for some unexplainable reason, knew she would not do that.*

They stood for a moment looking into each other's eyes and the look was like a kind of love-making too. It was very strange and the moment would afterward give him much to think about. In the future no doubt his life was to be filled with many thoughts. There was this woman he did not know at all, standing before him, and in their own way he and she were being lovers too. Had the thing not happened between himself and Natalie so recently, had he not still been filled with that, something of the sort might well have happened between him and this woman.

In reality the matter of the two people standing thus and looking at each other occupied but a moment. Then she sat down, a little confused, and he went quickly out.

There was a kind of joy in him now. "There is love abundant in the world. It may take many roads to expression. The woman in there is hungry for love and there is something fine and generous about her. She knows Natalie and I love and she has, in some obscure way I can't yet understand, given herself to that until it has become almost a physical experience with her too. There are a thousand things in life no one rightly understands. Love has as many branches as a tree."

He went up into a business street of the town and turned into a section with which he was not very familiar. He was passing a little store, near a Catholic church, such a store as is patronized by devout Catholics and in which are sold figures of the Christ on the cross, the Christ lying at the foot of the cross with His bleeding wounds, the Virgin standing with arms crossed looking demurely down, blessed candles, candlesticks, and the like. For a moment he stood before the store window looking at the figures displayed and then went in and bought a small framed picture of the Virgin, a supply of yellow candles, and two glass candlesticks, made in the shape of crosses and with little gilded figures of the Christ on the cross upon them.

To tell the truth the figure of the Virgin looked not unlike Natalie.* There was a kind of quiet strength in her. She stood, holding a lily in her right hand and the thumb and first finger of her left hand touched lightly a great heart pinned to her breast by a dagger. Across the heart was a wreath of five red roses.

John Webster stood for a moment looking into the Virgin's eyes and then bought the things and hurried out of the store. Then he took a street car and went to his own house. His wife and daughter were out and he went up into his own room and put the packages in a closet. When he came downstairs the servant Katherine was waiting for him. "May I get you something to eat again to-day?" she asked and smiled.

He did not stay to have lunch, but it was fine, being asked to stay. At any rate she had remembered the day when she had stood near him while he ate. He had liked being alone with her that day. Perhaps she had felt the same thing and had liked being with him.

He walked straight out of town and got into a country road and presently turned off the road into a small wood. For two hours he sat on a log looking at the trees now flaming with color.* The sun shone brightly and after a time the squirrels and birds became less conscious of his presence and the animal and bird life that had been stilled by his coming was renewed.

It was the afternoon after the night of his walking in the streets between the rows of houses the walls of which had been torn away by his fancy. "I shall tell Natalie of that to-night and I shall tell her also of what I intend to do at home there in my room. I shall tell her and she will say nothing.* She is a strange one. When she does not understand she believes. There is something in her that accepts life as these trees do," he thought.

III

A STRANGE kind of nightly ceremony was begun in John Webster's corner room on the second floor of his house. When he had come into the house he went softly upstairs and into his own room. Then he took off all his clothes and hung them in a closet. When he was quite nude he got out the little picture of the Virgin and set it up on a kind of dresser that stood in a corner between the two windows. On the dresser he also placed the two candlesticks with the Christ on the cross on them and putting two of the yellow candles in them lighted the candles.

As he had undressed in the darkness he did not see the room or himself until he saw by the light of the candles. Then he began to walk back and forth, thinking such thoughts as came into his head.

"I have no doubt I am insane," he told himself, "but as long as I am it might as well be a purposeful insanity. I haven't been liking this room or the clothes I wear. Now I have taken the clothes off and perhaps I can in some way purify the room a bit. As for my walking about in the streets and letting my fancy play over many people in their houses, that will be all right in its turn too, but at present my problem lies in this house. There have been

85

many years of stupid living in the house and in this room. Now I shall keep up this ceremony; making myself nude and walking up and down here before the Virgin, until neither my wife nor my daughter can keep up her silence. They will break in here some night quite suddenly and then I will say what I have to say before I go away with Natalie."

"As for you, my Virgin, I dare say I shall not offend you," he said aloud, turning and bowing to the woman within her frame. She looked steadily at him as Natalie might have looked and he kept smiling at her. It seemed quite clear to him now what his course in life was to be. He reasoned it all out slowly. In a way he did not, at the time, need much sleep. Just letting go of himself, as he was doing, was a kind of resting.

In the meantime he walked naked and with bare feet up and down the room trying to plan out his future life. "I accept the notion that I am at present insane and only hope I shall remain so," he told himself. After all, it was quite apparent that the sane people about were not getting such joy out of life as himself. There was this matter of his having brought the Virgin into his own naked presence and having set her up under the candles. For one thing the candles spread a soft glowing light through the room. The clothes he habitually wore and that he had learned to dislike because they had been made not for himself, but for some impersonal being, in some clothing factory, were now hung away, out of sight in the closet. "The gods have been good to me. I am not very young any more, but for some reason I have not let my body get fat or gross," he thought going into the circle of candle-light and looking long and earnestly at himself.

In the future and after the nights when his walking thus back and forth in the room had forced itself upon the attention of his wife and daughter until they were compelled to break in upon him, he would take Natalie with him and go away. He had provided himself with a little money, enough so that they could live for a few months. The rest would be left to his wife and daughter. After he and Natalie had got clear of the town they would go off somewhere, perhaps to the West. Then they would settle down somewhere and work for their living.

What he himself wanted, more than anything else, was to give way to the impulses within himself. "It must have been that, when I was a boy and my imagination played madly over all the life about me, I was intended to be something other than the dull clod I have been all these years. In Natalie's presence, as in the presence of a tree or a field, I can be myself. I dare say I shall have to be a little careful sometimes as I do not want to be declared insane and locked up somewhere, but Natalie will help me in that. In a way my letting go of myself will be an expression for both of us. In her own way she also has been locked within a prison. Walls have been erected about her too.

"It may just be, you see, that there is something of the poet in me and Natalie should have a poet for a lover.

"The truth is that I shall be at the job of in some way bringing grace and meaning into my life. It must be after all that it is for something of the sort life is intended.

"In reality it would not be such a bad thing if, in the few years of life I have left, I accomplish nothing of importance. When one comes right down to it accomplishment is not the vital thing in a life.

"As things are now, here in this town and in all the other towns and cities I have ever been in, things are a good deal in a muddle. Everywhere lives are lived without purpose. Men and women either spend their lives going in and out of the doors of houses and factories or they own houses and factories and they live their lives and find themselves at last facing death and the end of life without having lived at all."

He kept smiling at himself and his own thoughts as he walked up and down the room and occasionally he stopped walking and made an elaborate bow to the Virgin. "I hope you are a true virgin," he said. "I brought you into this room and into the presence of my nude body because I thought you would be that. You see, being a virgin, you cannot have anything but pure thoughts."

IV

Quite often, during the day-time, and after the time when the nightly ceremony in his room began, John Webster had moments of fright. "Suppose," he thought, "my wife and daughter should look through the keyhole into my room some night, and should decide to have me locked up instead of coming in here and giving me the chance I want to talk with them. As the matter stands I cannot carry out my plans unless I can get the two of them into the room without asking them to come."

He had a keen sense of the fact that what was to transpire in his room would be terrible for his wife. Perhaps she would not be able to stand it. A streak of cruelty had developed in him. In the day-time now he seldom went to his office and when he did, stayed but a few minutes. Every day he took a long walk in the country, sat under the trees, wandered in woodland paths and in the evening walked in silence beside Natalie, also in the country. The days marched past in quiet fall splendor.* There was a kind of sweet new responsibility in just being alive when one felt so alive.

One day he climbed a little hill from the top of which he could see, off across fields, the factory chimneys of his town. A soft haze lay over woodland and fields. The voices within him did not riot now, but chattered softly.

As for his daughter, the thing to be done was to startle her, if possible, into a realization of the fact of life. "I owe her that," he thought. "Even though the thing that must happen will be terribly hard for her mother it may bring life to Jane. In the end the dead must surrender their places in life to the living. When long ago, I went to bed of that woman, who is my Jane's mother, I took a certain responsibility upon myself. The going to bed of her may not have been the most lovely thing in the world, as it turned out, but it is a thing that was done and the result is this child, who is now no longer a child, but who has become in her physical life a woman. Having helped to give her this physical life I have now to try at least to give her this other, this inner life also."

He looked down across the fields toward the town. When the job he had yet to do was done he would go away and spend the rest of his life moving about among people, looking at people, thinking of them and their lives. Perhaps he would become a writer. That would be as it turned out.

He got up from his seat on the grass at the top of the hill and went down along a road that would lead back to town and to his evening's walk with Natalie. Evening would be coming on soon now. "I'll never preach at anyone, anyhow. If by chance I do ever become a writer I'll only try to tell people what I have seen and heard in life and besides that I'll spend my time walking up and down, looking and listening," he thought.

BOOK THREE

I

AND on that very night, after he had been seated
on the hill thinking of his life and what he would
do with what remained of it and after he had
gone for the customary evening walk with Natalie,
the doors of his room did open and his wife and
daughter came in.

It was about half past eleven o'clock and for an
hour he had been walking softly up and down before
the picture of the Virgin. The candles were
lighted. His feet made a soft cat-like sound on the
floor. There was something strange and startling
about hearing the sound in the quiet house.

The door leading to his wife's room opened and
she stood looking at him. Her tall form filled the
door-way and her hands clutched at the sides of the
door. She was very pale and her eyes were fixed
and staring. "John," she said hoarsely and then
repeated the word. She seemed to want to say
more, but to be unable to speak. There was a
sharp sense of ineffectual struggle.

It was certain she was not very handsome as she
stood there. "Life pays people out. Turn your
back on life and it gets even with you. When people
do not live they die and when they are dead they
look dead," he thought. He smiled at her and

93

then turned his head away and stood listening.

It came—the sound for which he was listening. There was a stir in his daughter's room. He had counted so much on things turning out as he wished and had even had a premonition it would happen on this particular night. What had happened he thought he understood. For more than a week now there had been this storm raging over the ocean of silence that was his wife. There had been just such another prolonged and resentful silence after their first attempt at love-making and after he had said certain sharp hurtful things to her. That had gradually worn itself out, but this new thing was something different. It could not wear itself out in that way. The thing had happened for which he had prayed. She had been compelled to meet him here, in the place he had prepared.

And now his daughter, who had also been lying awake night after night, and hearing the strange sounds in her father's room, would be compelled to come. He felt almost gay. On that evening he had told Natalie that he thought his struggle might come to a breaking point that night and had asked her to be ready for him. There was a train that would leave town at four in the morning. "Perhaps we shall be able to take that," he had said.

"I'll be waiting for you,"*Natalie had said and now there was his wife, standing pale and trembling, as though about to fall and looking from the Virgin between her candles to his naked body and then there was the sound of some one moving in his daughter's room.

And now her door crept open an inch, softly, and he went at once and threw it completely open. "Come in," he said. "Both of you come in. Go sit there on the bed together. I've something to say to you both." There was a commanding ring in his voice.

There was no doubt the women were both, for the moment at least, completely frightened and cowed. How pale they both were. The daughter put her hands to her face and ran across the room to sit upright holding to a railing at the foot of the bed and still holding one hand over her eyes and his wife walked across and fell face downward on the bed. She made a continuous little moaning sound for a time and then buried her face in the bed-clothes and became silent. There was no doubt both women thought him completely insane.

John Webster began walking up and down before them. "What an idea," he thought looking down at his own bare legs. He smiled, again looking into the frightened face of his daughter. "Hito, tito,"* he whispered to himself. "Now do not lose your head. You're going to pull this off. Keep your head on your shoulders, my boy." Some strange freak of his mind made him raise his two hands as though he were conferring some kind of blessing upon the two women. "I'm off my nut, out of my shell, but I don't care at all," he mused.*

He addressed his daughter. "Well, Jane," he began, speaking with great earnestness and in a clear quiet voice, "I can see you are frightened and upset by what is going on here and I do not blame you.

95

The truth is that it was all planned. For a week now you have been lying awake in your bed in the next room there and hearing me move about in here and in that room over there your mother has been lying. There is something I have been wanting to say to you and your mother, but as you know there has never been any habit of talk in this house.

"The truth is I have wanted to startle you and I guess I have succeeded in that."

He walked across the room and sat on the bed between his daughter and the heavy inert body of his wife. They were both dressed in nightgowns and his daughter's hair had fallen down about her shoulders. It was like his wife's hair when he married her. Then her hair had been just such a golden yellow and when the sun shone on it coppery and brown lights sometimes appeared.

"I'm going away from this house to-night. I'm not going to live with your mother any more," he said, leaning forward and looking at the floor.

He straightened his body and for a long time sat looking at his daughter's body. It was young and slender. She would not be extraordinarily tall like her mother but would be a woman of the medium height. He studied her body carefully. Once, when she was a child of six, Jane had been ill for nearly a year and he remembered now that during that time she had been very precious to him. It was during a year when the business had gone badly and he thought he might have to go into bankruptcy at any moment, but he had managed to keep a trained nurse in the house during the whole period of her illness. Every day during that time he came home from the factory at noon and went into his daughter's room.

There was no fever. What was wrong? He had thrown the bedclothes off the child's body and had looked at it. She was very thin then and the little bones of the body could be plainly seen. There was just the tiny bony structure over which the fair white skin was drawn.

The doctors had said it was a matter of malnutrition, that the food given the child did not nourish it, and they couldn't find the right food.* The mother had been unable to nurse the child. Sometimes during that period he stood for long minutes looking at the child whose tired listless eyes looked back at him. The tears ran from his own eyes.

It was very strange. Since that time and after she had suddenly begun to grow well and strong again he had in some way lost all track of his daughter. Where had he been in the meantime and where had she been? They were two people and they had been living in the same house all these years.* What was it that shut people off from each other? He looked carefully at his daughter's body, now clearly outlined under the thin nightgown. She had rather broad hips, like a woman's hips, and her shoulders were narrow.* How her body trembled. How afraid she was. "I am a stranger to her and it is not surprising," he thought. He leaned forward and looked at her bare feet. They were small and well made. Sometime a lover would come to kiss them.* Sometime a man would feel

97

concerning her body as he now felt concerning the strong hard body of Natalie Swartz.

His silence seemed to have aroused his wife, who turned and looked at him. Then she sat up on the bed and he sprang to his feet and stood confronting her. "John," she said again in a hoarse whisper as though wishing to call him back to her out of some dark mysterious place. Her mouth opened and closed two or three times like the mouth of a fish taken out of the water. He looked away and paid no more attention to her and she again put her face down among the bedclothes.

"What I wanted, long ago, when Jane was a tiny thing, was simply that life come into*her and that is what I want now. That's all I do want. That's what I'm after now,'*John Webster thought.

He began walking up and down the room again, having a sense of great leisure. Nothing would happen. Now his wife had again fallen into the ocean of silence. She would lie there on the bed and say nothing, do nothing until he had finished saying what he had to say and had gone away. His daughter was blind and dumb with fear now, but perhaps he could warm the fear out of her.* "I must go about this matter slowly, take my time, tell her everything," he thought. The frightened girl now took her hand from before her eyes and looked at him. Her mouth trembled and then a word was formed. "Father," she said appealingly.

He smiled at her reassuringly and made a movement with his arm toward the Virgin, sitting so

98

solemnly between the two candles. "Look up there for a moment while I talk to you," he said.

He plunged at once into an explanation of his situation.

"There has been something broken," he said. "It is the habit of life in this house. Now you will not understand, but sometime you will.

"For years I have not been in love with this woman here, who is your mother and has been my wife, and now I have fallen in love with another woman. Her name is Natalie and to-night, after you and I have had our talk, she and I are going away to live together."

On an impulse he went and knelt on the floor at his daughter's feet and then quickly sprang up again. "No, that's not right. I am not to ask her forgiveness, I am to tell her of things," he thought.

"Well now," he began again, "you are going to think me insane and perhaps I am. I don't know. Anyway my being here in this room with the Virgin and without any clothes, the strangeness of all this will make you think me insane. Your mind will cling to that thought. It will want to cling to that thought," he said aloud. "It may turn out so for a time."

He seemed puzzled as to how to say all the things he wanted to say. The whole matter, the scene in the room, the talk with his daughter that he had planned so carefully was going to be a harder matter to handle than he had counted on.* He had thought there would be a kind of final significance in his nakedness and in the presence of the Virgin and her candles. Had he overset the stage? He wondered, and kept looking with eyes filled with anxiety at his daughter's face. It told him nothing. She was just frightened and clinging to the railing at the foot of the bed as one cast suddenly into the sea might cling to a floating piece of wood. His wife's body lying on the bed had a strange rigid look. Well there had for years been something rigid and cold in the woman's body. Perhaps she had died. That would be a thing to have happen. It would be something he had not counted upon. It was rather strange, now that he came to face the problem before him, how very little the presence of his wife had to do with the matter in hand.

He stopped looking at his daughter and began walking up and down and as he walked he talked. In a calm, although slightly strained voice he began trying to explain first of all the presence of the Virgin and the candles in the room. He was speaking now to some person, not his own daughter but just a human being like himself. Immediately he felt relieved. "Well, now. That's the ticket. That's the way to go at things," he thought. For a long time he went on talking and walking thus up and down. It was better not to think too much. One had to cling to the faith that the thing he had so recently found within himself and within Natalie was somewhere alive in her too. Before the morning when the whole matter between himself and Natalie began, his life had been like a beach covered with rubbish and lying in darkness. The beach was covered with old dead water-logged trees and stumps. The twisted roots of old trees stuck up into the darkness. Before it lay the heavy sluggish inert sea of life.

And then there had come this storm within and now the beach was clean. Could he keep it clean? Could he keep it clean so that it would sparkle in the morning light?

He was trying to tell his daughter Jane something about the life he had lived in the house with her and why, before he could talk to her, he had been compelled to do something extraordinary, like bringing the Virgin into his room and taking off his own body the clothes that, when he wore them, would make him seem in her eyes just the goer in and out of the house, the provider of bread and clothes for herself she had always known.

Speaking very clearly and slowly, as though afraid he would get off the track, he told her something of his life as a business man, of how little essential interest he always had in the affairs that had occupied all his days.

He forgot about the Virgin and for a time spoke only of himself. He came again to sit beside her and as he talked boldly put his hand on her leg. The flesh was cold under her thin nightgown.

"I was a young thing as you are now, Jane, when I met the woman who is your mother and who was my wife," he explained. "You must try to adjust your mind to the thought that both your mother and I were once young things like yourself.

"I suppose your mother, when she was your age

must have been very much as you are now. She would of course have been somewhat taller. I remember that her body was at that time very long and slender. I thought it very lovely then.

"I have cause to remember your mother's body. She and I first met each other through our bodies. At first there was nothing else, just our naked bodies. We had that and we denied it. Perhaps upon that everything might have been built, but we were too ignorant or too cowardly. It is because of what happened between your mother and myself that I have brought you into my own naked presence and have brought this picture of the Virgin in here. I have a desire to in some way make the flesh a sacred thing to you."

His voice had grown soft and reminiscent and he took his hand from his daughter's leg and touched her cheeks and then her hair. He was frankly making love to her now and she had somewhat fallen under his influence. He reached down and taking one of her hands held it tightly.

"We met, you see, your mother and I, at the house of a friend. Although, until a few weeks ago, when I suddenly began to love another woman, I had not for years thought about that meeting, it is, at this moment, as clear in my mind as though it had happened here, in this house, to-night.

"The whole thing, of which I now want to tell you the details, happened right here in this town, at the house of a man who was at that time my friend. Now he is dead, but at that time we were constantly together. He had a sister, a year younger than himself, of whom I was fond, but although we went about together a good deal, she and I were not in love with each other. Afterward she married and moved out of town.

"There was another young woman, the very woman who is now your mother, who was coming to that house to visit my friend's sister and as they lived at the other end of town and as my father and mother were away from town on a visit I was asked to visit there too. It was to be a kind of special occasion. The Christmas holidays were coming on and there were to be many parties and dances.

"A thing happened to me and your mother that was not at bottom so unlike the thing that has happened to you and me here to-night," he said sharply. He had grown a little excited again and thought he had better get up and walk. Dropping his daughter's hand he sprang to his feet and for a few minutes walked nervously about. The whole thing, the startled fear of him that kept going and coming in his daughter's eyes and the inert silent presence of his wife, was making what he wanted to do more difficult than he had imagined it would be. He looked at his wife's body lying silent and motionless on the bed. How many times he had seen the same body, lying just in that way. She had submitted to him long ago and had been submitting to the life in himself ever since. The figure his mind had made, 'an ocean of silence,' fitted her well. She had always been silent. At the best all she had learned from life was a half-resentful habit of submission. Even when she talked to him she did not really talk. It was odd indeed that Natalie out of her silence could say so many things to him while he and this woman in all their years together had said nothing really touching each other's lives.

He looked from the motionless body of the older woman to his daughter and smiled. "I can enter into her," he thought exultant. "She cannot shut me out of herself, does not want to shut me out of herself." There was something in his daughter's face that told him what was going on in her mind. The younger woman now sat looking at the figure of the Virgin and it was evident that the dumb fright that had taken such complete possession of her when she was ushered abruptly into the room and the presence of the naked man was beginning a little to loosen its grip. In spite of herself she was thinking. There was the man, her own father, moving nude like a tree in winter about the room and occasionally stopping to look at her, the dim light, the Virgin with the candles burning beneath and the figure of her mother lying on the bed. Her father was trying to tell her some story she wanted to hear. In some way it concerned herself, some vital part of herself. There was no doubt it was wrong, terribly wrong for the story to be told and for her to listen, but she wanted to hear it now.*

"After all I was right," John Webster was thinking. "Such a thing as has happened here might make or utterly ruin a woman of Jane's age, but as it is everything will come out right. She has a streak of cruelty in her too. There is a kind of health in her eyes now. She wants to know. After this experience she will perhaps no longer be afraid of the dead. It is the dead who are forever frightening the living."

He took up the thread of his tale as he walked up and down in the dim light.

"A thing happened to your mother and me. I went to my friend's house in the early morning and your mother was to arrive on a train in the late afternoon. There were two trains, one at noon and the other in the afternoon about five, and as she would have to get up in the middle of the night to take the first one we all supposed she would come later. My friend and I had planned to spend the day hunting rabbits on the fields near town and we got back to his house about four.

"There would be time enough for us to bathe and dress ourselves before the guest arrived. When we got home my friend's mother and sister had gone out and we supposed there was no one in the house but a servant. In reality the guest, you see, had arrived on the train at noon, but that we did not know and the servant did not tell us. We hurried upstairs to undress and then went downstairs and into a shed to bathe. At that time people had no bathtubs in their houses and the servant had filled two washtubs with water and had put them in the shed. After she had filled the tubs she disappeared, got herself out of the way.

"We were running about the house naked as I am doing here now. What happened was that I came naked out of that shed downstairs and climbed the stairs to the upper part of the house, going to my room. The day had grown warm and now it was almost dark."

Again John Webster came to sit with his daughter on the bed and to hold one of her hands.

"I went up the stairs and along a hallway and opening a door went across a room to what I thought was my bed, where I had laid out the clothes I had brought that morning in my bag.

"You see what had happened was that your mother had got out of bed in her own town at midnight on the night before and when she arrived at my friend's house his mother and sister had insisted she undress and get into bed. She had not unpacked her bag, but had thrown off her clothes and had got in between the sheets as naked as I was when I walked in upon her. As the day had turned warm she had I suppose grown somewhat restless and in stirring about had thrown the bedclothes to one side.

"She lay, you see, quite nude on the bed, in the uncertain light, and as I had no shoes on my feet I made no sound when I came in to her.

"It was an amazing moment for me. I had walked directly to the bed and there she was within a few inches of my hands as they hung by my side. It was your mother's most lovely moment with me. As I have said she was then very slender and her long body was white like the sheets of the bed. At that time I had never before been in the presence of a woman undressed. I had just come from the bath. It was like a kind of wedding, you see.

"How long I stood there looking at her I don't know, but anyway she knew I was there. Her eyes

106

came up to me out of sleep like a swimmer out of the sea. Perhaps, it is just possible, she had been dreaming of me or of some other man.

"At any rate and for just a moment she was not frightened or startled at all. It was really our wedding moment, you see.

"O, had we only known how to live up to that moment! I stood there looking at her and she was there on the bed looking at me. There must have been a glowing something alive in our eyes. I did not know then all I felt, but long afterward, sometimes, when I was walking in the country or riding on a train, I thought. Well, what did I think? It was evening you see. I mean that afterward, sometimes, when I was alone, when it was evening and I was alone I looked off across hills or I saw a river making a white streak down below as I stood on a cliff. What I mean to say is that I have spent all these years trying to recapture that moment and now it is dead."

John Webster threw out his hands with a gesture of disgust and then got quickly off the bed. His wife's body had begun to stir and now she lifted herself up. For a moment her rather huge figure was crouched on the bed and she looked like some great animal on all fours, sick and trying to get up and walk.

And then she did get up, putting her feet firmly on the floor and walking slowly out of the room without looking at the two people. Her husband stood with his back pressed against the wall of the room and watched her go. "Well, that's the end of her," he thought grimly. The door that led into her room came slowly toward him. Now it was closed. "Some doors have to be closed forever too," he told himself.

He was still in his daughter's presence and she was not afraid of him. He went to a closet and getting out his clothes began to dress. That he realized was a terrible moment. Well, he was playing the cards he held in his hand to the limit. He had been nude. Now he had to get into his clothes, into the clothes he had come to feel had no meaning and were altogether unlovely because the unknown hands that had fashioned them were unmoved by the desire to create beauty.* An absurd notion came to him. "Has my daughter a sense of moments? Will she help me now?" he asked himself.

And then his heart jumped. His daughter Jane had done a quite lovely thing. While he jerked his clothes on hurriedly she turned and threw herself face downward on the bed, in the same position in which her mother had been but a moment before.*

"I walked out of her room into the hallway," he explained. "My friend had come upstairs and was standing in the hallway lighting a lamp that was fastened to a bracket on the wall. You can perhaps imagine the things that were going through my mind. My friend looked at me, as yet knowing nothing. You see, he did not yet know that woman was in the house, but he had seen me walk out of the room. He had just lighted the lamp when I came out and closed the door behind me and the light fell on my face. There must have been something that startled him. Later we never spoke of the matter at all. As it turned out every one was embarrassed and made self-conscious by what had occurred and what was still to occur.

"I must have walked out of the room like a man walking in sleep. What was in my mind? What had been in my mind when I stood there beside her naked body and even before that? It was a situation that might not occur again in a lifetime. You have just now seen how your mother went out of this room. You are wondering, I dare say, what is in her mind. I can tell you of that. There is nothing in her mind. She has made her mind a blank empty place into which nothing that matters can come. She has spent a lifetime at that, as I dare say most people have.

"As for that evening when I stood in the hallway, with the light of that lamp shining on me and with my friend looking and wondering what was the matter—that, after all, is what I must try to tell you about."

He was partially dressed now and again Jane was sitting upright on the bed. He came to sit in his shirt sleeves beside her. Long afterward she remembered how extraordinarily young he looked at that moment. He seemed intent on making her understand fully everything that had happened. "Well, you understand," he said slowly, "that although she had seen my friend and his sister before, she had never seen me. At the same time she knew I was to stay in the house during her visit.

No doubt she had been having thoughts about the strange young man she was to meet and it is also true I had been having thoughts about her.

"Even at the moment when I walked, thus nude, into her presence she was a living thing in my mind. And when she came up to me, out of sleep you see, before she had time to think, I was a living thing to her then. What living things we were to each other we dared understand but for a moment. I know that now, but for many years after that happened I didn't know and was only confused.

"I was confused also when I came out into the hallway and stood before my friend. You understand that he did not yet know she was in the house. I had to tell him something and it was like having to tell in some public way the secret of what happens between two people in a moment of love.

"It can't be done, you understand, and so there I stood stammering and making things worse every minute. I must have had a guilty look on my face and right away I began to feel guilty, although when I was in that room standing by the bed, as I have explained, I didn't feel guilty at all, quite the contrary in fact.

" 'I went naked into that room and stood beside the bed and that woman is in there now, all naked,' I said.

"My friend was of course amazed. 'What woman?' he asked.

"I tried to explain. 'Your sister's friend. She is in there naked on the bed and I went in and stood beside her. She came on the train at noon,' I said.

"You see, I appeared to know all about everything. I felt guilty. That was what was the matter with me. I suppose I stammered and acted confused. 'He'll never believe it was an accident now. He'll think I am up to something strange,' I thought immediately. Whether he ever had all or any of the thoughts that went through my mind at that moment and of which I was in a way accusing him I never found out. I was always a stranger in that house after that moment. You see, what I had done, to have been made quite clear would have required a good deal of whispered explanation that I never offered and, even after your mother and I were married, things were never as they had been between me and my friend.

"And so I stood there stammering and he was looking at me with a puzzled startled look in his eyes. The house was very quiet and I remember how the light of the lamp, in its bracket on the wall, fell on our two naked bodies. My friend, the man who was the witness of that moment of vital drama in my life, is dead now. He died some eight years ago and your mother and I dressed ourselves in our best clothes and went in a carriage to his funeral and later to a graveyard to watch his body being put away into the ground, but at that moment he was very much alive and I shall always continue to think of him as he was then. We had been tramping about all day in the fields and he, like myself, had just come, you remember, from the bath. His young body was very slender and strong and it made a glowing white mark against the dark wall of the hallway, against which he stood.

"Were we both expecting something more to happen, waiting for something more to happen? We did not speak to each other again, but stood in silence. Perhaps he was only startled by my statement of what I had just done and by something a little strange in the manner in which I had told him.* Ordinarily after such an accident there would have been a kind of giggling confusion, the thing would have been passed off as a kind of secret and delicious joke, but I had killed all possibility of its being taken in that spirit*by something in the way I had looked and acted when I came out to him. I was, I suppose, at the same time both too conscious and not conscious enough of the significance of what I had done.

"And so we just stood in silence looking at each other and then the door downstairs, that led to the street, opened and his mother and sister came into the house. They had taken advantage of the fact that their guest had gone to sleep and had walked to the business part of town to do some shopping.

"As for myself, what was going on within me at that moment is the hardest thing of all to explain. I had difficulty getting hold of myself, of that you may be sure. What I think now, at this moment, is that then, at that moment long ago when I stood there naked in that hallway beside my friend, something had gone out of me that I could not immediately get back.

"Perhaps when you have grown older you will understand as you cannot understand now."

John Webster looked long and hard at his daughter who also looked at him. For both of them the story he was telling had become a rather impersonal one. The woman, who was so closely connected to them both as wife and mother, had gone quite out of the tale as she had but a few moments before gone stumbling out of the room.

"You see," he said slowly, "what I did not then understand, could not then have been expected to understand, was that I had really gone out of myself in love to the woman on the bed in the room. No one understands that a thing of that sort may occur like a thought flashing across the mind. What I am nowadays coming to believe and would like to get fixed in your mind, young woman, is that such moments come into all lives, but that in all the millions of people who are born and live long or short lives but a few ever really come to find out what life is like. There is a kind of perpetual denial of life, you understand.

"I was dazed as I stood in the hallway outside that woman's room long ago. There had been a flashing kind of something between the woman and myself, in the moment I have described to you, when she came up to me out of sleep. Something deep in our two beings had been touched and I could not quickly recover. There had been a marriage, something intensely personal to our two selves, and by chance it had been made a kind of public affair. I

113

suppose it would have turned out the same way had we two been alone in the house. We were very young. Sometimes I think all the people in the world are very young. They cannot carry the fire of life when it flashes to life in their hands.

"And in the room, behind the closed door, the woman must have been having, at just that moment, some such feeling as myself. She had raised herself up and was now sitting on the edge of the bed. She was listening to the sudden silence of the house as my friend and I were listening. It may be an absurd thing to say, but it is nevertheless true that my friend's mother and sister, who had just come into the house, were both, in some unconscious way, affected also as they stood with their coats on downstairs, also listening.

"Just then, at that moment, in the room in the darkness, the woman began to sob like a broken-hearted child. There had been a thing quite tremendous come to her and she could not hold it. To be sure the immediate cause of her weeping that way, the way in which she would have explained her grief, was shame. That was what she thought had happened to her, that she had been put into a shameful ridiculous position. She was a young girl. I dare say thoughts had already come into her mind concerning what all the others would think. At any rate I know that at the moment and afterward I was more pure than herself.

"The sound of her sobbing rang through the house and downstairs my friend's mother and sister, who had been standing and listening as I have said, now ran to the foot of the stairway leading up.

"As for myself, I did what must have seemed to all the others a ridiculous, almost a criminal thing. I ran to the door leading into the bedroom and tearing it open ran in, slamming the door behind me. It was by this time almost completely dark in the room, but without hesitation I ran to her. She was sitting on the edge of the bed and as she sobbed her body rocked back and forth. She was, at that moment, like a slender young tree, standing in an open field, without any other trees to protect it. She was shaken as by a great storm, that's what I mean.

"And so you see, I ran to her and threw my arms about her body.

"The thing that had happened to us before happened once again, for the last time in our lives. She gave herself to me, that's what I am trying to say. There was another marriage. For just a moment she became altogether quiet and in the uncertain light her face was turned up to mine. From her eyes came that same look, as of one coming up to me, out of a deep buried place, out of the sea or something like that. I have always thought of the place out of which she came as the sea.

"I dare say if anyone but you heard me tell this and if I had told it to you under less strange circumstances you would only have thought me a romantic fool. 'She was startled,' you would say and I dare say she was. But also there was this other. Even though it was dark in the room I felt the thing glowing deep down in her and then coming up, straight up to me. The moment was unspeakably lovely. It lasted for but a fraction of a second, like the snapping of the shutter of a camera, and then it passed.

"I still held her tightly and the door opened and in the doorway stood my friend and his mother and sister. He had taken the lamp from its bracket on the wall and held it in his hand. She sat quite naked on the bed and I stood beside her, with one knee on the edge of the bed, and with my arms thrown about her." *

II

TEN or fifteen minutes had passed and in the interval John Webster had completed his arrangements for leaving the house and setting out with Natalie on his new adventure in life. In a short time now he would be with her and all the cords that bound him to his old life would have been cut. It was sure that, whatever happened, he would never see his wife again and perhaps he would never see again the woman, now in the room with him, who was his daughter. If the doors of life could be torn open they could also be closed. One could walk out of a certain phase of life as out of a room. There might be traces of him left behind, but he would no longer be there.

He had put on his collar and coat, arranging everything quite calmly. Also he had packed a small bag, putting in extra shirts, pajamas, toilet articles, et cetera.

During all this time his daughter sat at the foot of the bed with her face buried in the crook of her arm that hung over the railing of the bed. Was she thinking? Were voices talking within her? What was she thinking?

In the interval, when*the father's telling of the tale of his life in the house had ceased and while he was doing the necessary little mechanical things before setting out on his new way of life, there was this pregnant time of silence.

There was no doubt that, if he had become insane, the insanity within was becoming constantly more fixed, more a habit of his being. There was, taking constantly deeper and deeper roots within him, a new viewpoint of life or rather to be a bit fancy and speak of the matter more in the modern spirit, as he himself might later have done laughingly, one might say he had been permanently caught up and held by a new rhythm of life.*

At any rate it is true that, long afterward, when the man sometimes spoke of the experiences of that time, what he himself said was that one, by an effort of his own, and if he would but dare let himself go, could almost at will walk in and out of various planes of life. In speaking of such matters later he sometimes gave the impression that he quite calmly believed that one, once he had acquired the talent and courage for it, that one might even go so far as to be able to walk in the air along a street at the level of the second story of houses and look in at the people going about their private affairs in the upper rooms as a certain historic man of the East is said to have once walked on the surface of the waters of a sea. It was all a part of a notion he had got fixed in his head regarding the tearing down of walls and the taking of people out of prisons.

There he was, at any rate, in his room fixing, let us say, his tie pin in his necktie. He had got out the small bag into which he put as he thought of them, the things he might need.* In the next room his wife, the woman who in the process of living her life had become the large heavy inert one, was lying in silence on her bed as she had but a short while before been lying on the bed in the presence of himself and his daughter.

What dark and terrible things were in her mind? Or was her mind a blank as John Webster sometimes thought it had become?

At his back, in the same room with himself, was his daughter, in her thin nightgown and with her hair fallen down about her face and shoulders. Her body—he could see the reflection of it in the glass as he arranged the tie—was drooped and limp. The experiences of the evening had no doubt taken something out of her body, perhaps permanently. He wondered about that and his eyes in roving about the room found again the Virgin with the candles burning by her side looking calmly at the scene. It was that calmness men worshipped in the Virgin perhaps. It was a strange turn of events that had led him to bring her, the calm one, into the room, to make her a part of the whole remarkable affair. No doubt it was the calm virginal thing he was at that moment in the process of taking out of his daughter, it was the coming of that element out of her body that had left her so limp and apparently lifeless. There was no doubt he had been daring. The hand that was arranging the tie trembled a little.

Doubt came. As I have said the house was at

that moment very silent. In the next room his wife, lying on the bed, made no sound. She floated in a sea of silence, as she had done ever since that other night, long before, when shame, in the form of a naked and distraught man, had embraced her nakedness in the presence of those others.

Had he in turn done the same thing to his daughter? Had he plunged her also into that sea? It was a startling and terrible thought. One did no doubt upset things by becoming insane in a sane world or sane in an insane world. Quite suddenly everything became upset, turned quite upside down.

And then it might well be true that the whole matter simply resolved itself into this—that he, John Webster, was merely a man who had become suddenly enamoured of his stenographer and wanted to go and live with her and that he had found himself without the courage to do so simple a thing without making a fuss about it, without in fact an elaborate justification of himself, at the expense of these others. To justify himself he had devised this strange business of appearing nude before the young girl who was his daughter and who in reality, being his daughter, deserved the utmost consideration from him. There was no doubt but that, from one point of view, what he had done was altogether unforgivable. "After all I am still but a washing machine manufacturer in a small Wisconsin town," he told himself, whispering the words out slowly and distinctly to himself.

That was a thing to bear in mind. Now his bag was packed and he was quite dressed and ready to set out. When the mind no longer moved forward sometimes the body took its place and made the consummation of an act once begun quite definitely unavoidable.

He walked across the room and stood for a time looking up into the calm eyes of the Virgin in the frame.

His thoughts were again like bells heard ringing across fields. "I am in a room in a house on a street in a town in the state of Wisconsin. At this moment most of the other people here in town, the people among whom I have always lived, are in bed and asleep but to-morrow morning, when I am gone, the town will be here and will move forward with its life, as it has been doing since I was a young fellow, married a woman and began living my present life." There were these definite facts of existence. One wore clothes, ate, moved about among his fellow men and women. Certain phases of life were lived in the darkness of nights, others in the light of days. In the morning the three women who worked at his office and also the book-keeper would appear to do their usual tasks. When, after a time, neither he nor Natalie Swartz appeared there would begin a looking from one to another. After a time whispering would begin. There would begin a whispering that would run through the town, visit all the houses, the shops, the stores. Men and women would stop on the street to speak to each other, the men speaking to other men, the women to other women. The women who were wives would be a little angry at him and the men a little envious, but the men would perhaps speak of him more bitterly than the women. That would be to cover up their own wish to break in some way the boredom of their own existence.

A smile spread itself over John Webster's face and it was then he went to sit on the floor at his daughter's feet and tell her the rest of the story of his married life. There was after all a kind of wicked satisfaction to be got out of his situation. As for his daughter, well, it was a fact too, that nature had made the connection between them quite inevitable. He might throw into his daughter's lap the new aspect of life that had come to him and then, did she choose to reject it, that would be a matter for her to decide. People would not blame her. "Poor girl," they would say, "what a shame she should have had such a man for a father." On the other hand and if after hearing all he had to say she decided to run a little more swiftly through life, to open her arms to it, in a way of speaking, what he had done would be a help. There was Natalie whose old mother had made herself a great nuisance by getting drunk and shouting so that all the neighbors could hear and calling her hard-working daughters whores. It was perhaps absurd to think that such a mother might be giving her daughters a better chance in life than a quite respectable mother could possibly have given them and still, in a world upset, turned upside down as it were, that might be quite true too.

At any rate there was a quiet sureness in Natalie that was, even in his moments of doubt, amazingly quieting and healing to himself. "I love her and I accept her. If her old mother, by letting go of herself and shouting in the streets in a kind of drunken splendor*of abandonment, has made a clear way in which Natalie may walk, all hail to her too," he thought, smiling at his own thoughts.

He sat at his daughter's feet talking quietly and as he talked something within her became more quiet. She listened with constantly growing interest, looking down at him occasionally. He sat very close to her and occasionally leaned over a little and laid his cheek against her leg. "The devil! He was quite apparently making love to her too." She did not think such a thought definitely. A subtle feeling of confidence and sureness went out of him into her. He began the tale of his marriage again.

On the evening of his youth, when his friend and his friend's mother and sister had come into the presence of himself and the woman he was to marry, he had suddenly been overcome by the same thing that afterward left so permanent a scar on her. Shame swept over him.

Well what was he to do? How was he to explain this second running into that room and into the presence of the naked woman? It was a matter that could not be explained. A mood of desperation swept over him and he ran past the people at the door and down the hallway, this time getting into the room to which he had been assigned.

He had closed and locked the door behind him and then he dressed, hurriedly, with feverish rapidity. When he was quite dressed he came out of the room carrying his bag. The hallway was silent and the lamp had been put back into its bracket on the wall. What had happened? No doubt the daughter of the house was with the woman, trying to comfort her. His friend had perhaps gone into his own room and was at the moment dressing and no doubt thinking thoughts too. There was bound to be no end of disturbed agitated thinking in the house. Everything might have been all right had he not gone into the room that second time, but how could he ever explain that the second going was as unpremeditated as the first. He went quickly downstairs.

Below he met his friend's mother, a woman of fifty. She stood in a doorway that led into a dining room. A servant was putting dinner on the table. The laws of the household were being observed. It was time to dine and in a few minutes the people of the house would dine. "Holy Moses," he thought, "I wonder if she could come down here now and sit at table with myself and the others, eating food? Can the habits of existence so quickly reassert themselves after so profound a disturbance?"

He put his bag down on the floor by his feet and looked at the older woman. "I don't know," he began, and stood looking at her and stammering. She was confused, as every one in that house must have been confused at that moment, but there was something in her, very kindly, that gave sympathy when it could not understand. She started to speak. "It was all an accident and there is nobody hurt," she started to say, but he did not wait*to listen. Picking up the bag he rushed out of the house.

What was to be done then? He had hurried across town to his own home and it was dark and silent. His father and mother had gone away. His grandmother, that is to say, his mother's mother, was very ill in another town and his father and mother had gone there. They might not return for several days. There were two servants employed in the house, but as the house was to be unoccupied they had been permitted to go away. Even the fires were out. He could not stay there, but would have to go to a hotel.

"I went into the house and put my bag down on the floor by the front door," he explained, and a shiver ran through his body as he remembered the dreariness of that evening long before. It was to have been an evening of gaiety. The four young people had planned to go to a dance and in anticipation of the figure he would cut with the new girl from another town, he had, in advance, worked himself up to a state of semi-excitement. The devil!— He had counted on finding in her the something—

well, what was it?—the something a young fellow is always dreaming of finding in some strange woman who is suddenly to come up to him out of nowhere and bring with her new life which she presents to him freely, asking nothing.* "You see, the dream is obviously an impossible one, but one has it in youth," he explained, smiling. All through the telling of this part of his story he kept smiling. Did his daughter uuderstand?* One couldn't question her understanding too closely. "The woman is to come clad in shining garments and with a calm smile on her face," he went on, building up his fanciful picture. "With what regal grace she carries herself and yet, you understand, she is not some impossible cold drawn-away thing either. There are many men standing about, all no doubt more deserving than yourself, but it is to you she comes, walking slowly, with her body all alive. She is the unspeakably beautiful Virgin, but there is something very earthy about her too. The truth is that she can be very cold and proud and drawn-away when anyone else but yourself is concerned, but in your presence the coldness all goes out of her.

"She comes toward you and her hand, that holds before her slender young body a golden tray, trembles a little. On the tray there is a box, small and cunningly wrought, and within it is a jewel, a talisman, that is for you. You are to take the jewel, set in a golden ring, out of the box and put in on your finger. It is nothing. The strange and beautiful woman has but brought it to you as a sign, before all the others, that she lays herself at your

126

feet. When your hand reaches forward and takes the jewel from the box her body begins to tremble and the golden tray falls to the floor making a loud rattling sound. Something terrific happens to all the others who have been witnesses of the scene. Of a sudden all the people present realize that you, whom they had always thought of as just an ordinary fellow, not, to tell the truth, as worthy as themselves, well, you see, they have been made, fairly forced, to realize your true self. Of a sudden there you stand before them all in your true colors,*quite revealed at last. There is a kind of radiant splendor comes out of you and fairly lights up the room where you, the woman, and all the others, the men and women of your own town you have always known and who have always thought they knew you, where they all stand looking and gasping with astonishment.

"It is a moment. The most unbelievable thing happens. There is a clock on the wall and it has been ticking, ticking, running out the span of your life and the lives of all the others. Outside the room, in which this remarkable scene takes place, there is a street with the activities of the street going on. Men and women are perhaps hurrying up and down, trains are coming in and going out of distant railroad stations, and even further away ships are sailing on many wide seas and great winds are disturbing the waters of seas.

"And suddenly all is stopped. It is a fact. On the wall the clock stops ticking, moving trains become dead and lifeless, people in the streets, who have started to say words to each other, stand now with their mouths open, on the seas winds no longer blow.

"For all life everywhere there is this hushed moment and, out of it all, the buried thing within you asserts itself. Out of the great stillness you step and take the woman into your arms. In a moment now all life can begin to move and be again, but after this moment all life forever will have been colored by this act of your own, by this marriage. It was for this marriage you and the woman were made."

All of which is perhaps going the extreme limit of fancifulness, as John Webster was careful to explain to Jane, and yet, there he was in the upper bedroom with his daughter, brought suddenly close to the daughter he had never known until that moment, and he was trying to speak to her of his feelings at the moment when, in his youth, he had once played the part of a supreme and innocent fool.

"The house was like a tomb, Jane," he said, and there was a break in his voice.*

It was evident the old boyhood dream was not yet dead. Even now, in his maturity, some faint perfume of it floated up to him as he sat on the floor at his daughter's feet. "The fires in the house had been out all day and outdoors it was getting colder," he began again. "All through the house there was that kind of damp coldness that always makes one think of death. You must remember that I had been thinking, and was still thinking, of

what I had done at my friend's house as the act of
an insane fool. Well, you see, our house was
heated by stoves and there was a small one in my
own room upstairs. I went into the kitchen, where
behind the kitchen stove, in a box, kindlings were
always kept, cut and ready, and taking out an armful started upstairs.

"In the hallway, in the darkness at the foot of
the stairs, my leg knocked against a chair and I put
the armful of kindlings down on the chair seat.
I stood in the darkness trying to think and not
thinking. 'I'm going to be sick perhaps,' I thought.
My self-respect was all gone and perhaps one
cannot think at such times.

"In the kitchen, above the kitchen stove, before
which my mother or our servant Adaline was always
standing when the house was alive and not dead as
it was now, just up there, where one could see it
over the women's heads, there was a small clock
and now that clock began making a sound as loud as
though some one were beating on sheets of iron with
big hammers. In the house next door some one was
talking steadily or maybe reading aloud. The wife
of the German who lived in the next house had
been ill in bed for months and perhaps now he was
trying to entertain her by reading some story.
The words came steadily, but in a broken way too.
What I mean is, that there would be a steady little
run of sounds, then it would be broken and then
begin again. Sometimes the voice would be raised
a little, for emphasis no doubt, and that was like a
kind of splash, as when the waves along a beach

all, for a long time, run to the same place clearly marked on the wet sand and then there comes one wave that goes far beyond all the others and splashes against the face of a rock.*

"You see perhaps the state I was in. It was, as I have said, very cold in the house and for a long time I stood in one spot, not moving at all and thinking I never wanted to move again. The voices from the distance, from the German's house next door, were like voices coming from some hidden buried place in myself.* There was one voice telling me I was a fool and that, after what had happened, I could never again hold up my head in the world, and another voice telling me I was not a fool at all, but for the time the first voice had all the best of the argument. What I did was to stand there in the cold and try to let the two voices fight it out without putting in my oar, but after a while, it may have been because I was so cold, I began to cry like a kid and that made me so ashamed I went to the front door quickly and got out of the house forgetting to put on my overcoat.

"Well, I had left my hat in the house too and there I was outside in the cold, bareheaded, and presently as I walked, keeping as much as I could in unfrequented streets, it began to snow.

"All right," I said to myself, "I know what I'll do. I'll go to their house and ask her to marry me."

"When I got there my friend's mother was not in sight and the three younger people were sitting in the parlor of the house. I looked in through a window and then, fearing I would lose my courage if I hesitated, went boldly up and knocked on the door. I was glad anyway they had felt that after what had happened they couldn't go to the dance and when my friend came and opened the door I said nothing, but walked directly into the room where the two girls sat.

"She was on a couch in a corner, where the light from a lamp on a table in the centre of the room fell on her but faintly, and I went directly to her. My friend had followed me into the room, but now I turned to him and his sister and asked them both to go out of the room. 'Something has happened here to-night that can't very well be explained and we must be left alone together for a few minutes,' I said making a motion with my hand to where she sat on the couch.

"When they went out I followed to the door and closed it after them.

"And so there I was in the presence of the woman who was later to be my wife. There was an odd kind of droopiness to her whole person as she sat on the couch. Her body had, in a way you see, slid down from its perch on the couch and now she was lying rather than sitting. What I mean is that her body was draped on the couch. It was like a garment thrown carelessly down there. That had happened since I had come into the room. I stood before it a moment and then got down on my knees. Her face was very pale, but her eyes were looking directly into mine.

" 'I did something very strange twice this

evening,' I said, turning my face away so that I no longer looked into her eyes. Her eyes frightened and disconcerted me, I suppose. That must have been it. I had a certain speech to make and wanted to go through with it. There were certain words I was about to say, but now I know that at the same moment other words and thoughts, having nothing to do with what I was saying, were going on down within me.

"For one thing I knew my friend and his sister were at that moment standing just outside the door of the room waiting and listening.

"What were they thinking? Well, never mind that.

"What was I thinking myself? What was the woman to whom I was about to propose marriage thinking about?

"I had come to the house bareheaded, you understand, and no doubt looking a little wild. Perhaps every one in that house thought I had gone suddenly out of my mind and it may be that in fact I had.

"At any rate I felt very calm and on that evening and for all these years, up to a short time ago, when I became in love with Natalie, I've always been a very calm man, or at least thought I was. I have dramatized myself that way. What I suppose is that death is always a very calm thing and I must, in a way, have been committing suicide on that evening.

"There had been, in the town, a few weeks before this happened, a scandal that had got into the courts and was written about guardedly in our weekly newspaper. It concerned a case of rape. A farmer, who had employed in his household a young girl, had sent his wife off to town to buy supplies and while she was gone had got the girl into the upper part of his house and had raped her, tearing her clothes off and even beating her before he forced her to acquiesce in his desires. Later he had been arrested and brought to town where, at the very time I was kneeling on the floor before the body of my future wife, he was in jail.

"I speak of the matter because, as I knelt there, I remember now, a thought crossed my mind connecting me with the man. 'I am also committing a rape' something within me said.

"To the woman, who was there before me, so cold and white, I said something else.

" 'You understand that, this evening, when I first came to you naked, it was an accident,' I said. 'I want you to understand that, but I want you also to understand that when I came to you the second time it was not an accident. I want you to understand everything quite fully and then I want to ask you to marry me, to consent to be my wife.'

"That was what I said and after I had said it took one of her hands in mine and, without looking at her, knelt there at her feet waiting for her to speak. Perhaps had she spoken then, even in condemnation of me, everything would have been all right.

"She said nothing. I understand now why she could not, but then I did not understand. I have always, I admit, been impatient. Time passed and

133

I waited. I was like one who has fallen from a great height into the sea and who feels himself going down and down, deeper and deeper. There is a great weight, you understand, pressing upon the man in the sea and he cannot breathe. What I suppose is that in the case of a man, falling thus into the sea, the force of his fall does after a time expend itself and he comes to a stop in his descent, and then suddenly begins again rising to the surface of the sea.

"And something of the sort happened to me. When I had been kneeling there for some little time, at her feet, I suddenly sprang up. Going to the door I threw it open and there, as I had expected, stood my friend and his sister. I must have appeared to them, at the moment, almost gay, perhaps they afterward thought it an insane gaiety. I cannot say as to that. After that evening I never went back to their house and my former friend and I began avoiding each other's presence. There was no danger that they would tell anyone what had happened—out of respect to their guest, you understand. The woman was safe as far as their talking was concerned.

"Anyway I stood before them and smiled. 'Your guest and I have got into a jam because of a series of absurd accidents that perhaps did not look like accidents and now I have asked her to marry me. She has not made up her mind about that,' I said, speaking very formally and turning from them and going out of the house and to my father's house where I quite calmly got my overcoat, my hat and

134

my bag.* 'I'll have to go to the hotel and stay until father and mother come home,' I thought. At any rate I knew that the affairs of the evening would not, as I had supposed earlier in the evening, throw me into a time of illness."

III

"I DO not mean to say that after that evening I did think more clearly, but after that day and its adventures other days and weeks did come marching along and, as nothing specially happened as a result of what I had done, I couldn't stay in the half-exalted state I was in then."

John Webster rolled over on the floor at his daughter's feet and, squirming about so that he lay on his belly facing her, looked up into her face. He had his elbows on the floor and his chin rested on his two hands. There was something diabolically strange about the way youth had come into his figure and he had quite won his way with his daughter. There he was, you see, wanting nothing specially from her and he was wholeheartedly giving himself to her. For the time even Natalie was forgotten and as for his wife, in the next room lying on the bed and perhaps in her dumb way suffering as he had never suffered, to him at the moment she simply did not*exist.

Well, there was the woman, who was his daughter, before him and he was giving himself to her. It is likely that at the moment he had quite forgotten she was his daughter. He was thinking now of his youth, when he was a young man, much perplexed by life, and was seeing her as a young woman who would inevitably, and as she went along through life, often be as perplexed as he had been. He tried to describe to her his feelings as a young man who had proposed to a woman who had made no answer and in whom nevertheless there was the perhaps romantic notion that he was in some queer way inevitably and finally attached to that particular woman.

"You see what I did then, Jane, is something you will perhaps find yourself doing some day and that it may be inevitable every one does." He reached forward and taking his daughter's bare foot in his hand drew it to him and kissed it. Then he sat quickly upright holding his knees in his arms. Something like a blush came swiftly over his daughter's face and then she began to look at him with very serious puzzled eyes. He smiled gaily.*

"And so you see, there I was, living right here in this very town and that girl to whom I had proposed marriage had gone away and I had heard nothing more from her. She only stayed at my friend's house a day or two after I had managed to make the beginning of her visit such a startling affair.

"For a long time my father had been scolding at me because I had taken no special interest in the washing machine factory, it was supposed I was after his day to take hold of and run, and so I decided I had better do a thing called 'settling down.' That is to say, I made up my mind it would be better for me if I gave myself less to dreams and to the kind of gawky youthfulness that only led to my doing such unaccountable things as that second running into that naked woman's presence.

"The truth is, of course, that my father, who in his own youth had come to a day when he had made just such another decision as I was then making, that he, for all his settling down and becoming a hard-working sensible man, hadn't got very much for it; but I didn't think of that at the time. Well, he wasn't such a gay old dog as I remember him now. He had always worked pretty hard, I suppose, and every day he sat for eight or ten hours at his desk and through all the years I had known him he had been subject to attacks of indigestion, during which every one in our house had to go softly about for fear of making his head ache worse than it did. The attacks used to come on about once a month and he would come home, and mother would fix him up on a couch in our front room, and she used to heat flatirons and roll them in towels and put them on his belly, and there he would lie all day groaning, and as you may suppose, making the life of our house a gay, festive affair.

"And then, when he got all right again and only looked a little gray*and drawn he would come sit at the table at meal-time with the rest of us and would talk to me about his life, as an entirely successful affair, and take it for granted I wanted just such another life.

"For some fool reason, I don't understand now, I thought then that was just what I did want. I suppose all the time I must have wanted something else and that made me spend so much of my time having vague dreams, but not only father, but all the older men in our town and perhaps in all the other towns along the railroad east and west were thinking and talking just that same way to their sons and I suppose I got caught up by the general drift of thinking and just went into it blind, with my head down, not thinking at all.

"So there I was, a young washing machine manufacturer, and I hadn't any woman, and since that affair at his house I didn't see my former friend with whom I used to try to talk of the vague, but nevertheless more colorful dreams of my idle hours. After a few months father sent me out on the road to see if I couldn't sell washing machines to merchants in small towns and sometimes I was successful and did sell some and sometimes I didn't.

"At night in the towns I used to walk about in the streets and sometimes I did get in with a woman, with a waitress from the hotel, or a girl I had picked up on the streets.

"We walked about under the trees along the residence streets of the town and when I was lucky I sometimes induced one of them to go with me to a little cheap hotel or into the darkness of the fields at the edge of the towns.

"At such times we talked of love and sometimes I was a good deal moved, but after all not really moved.

"The whole thing started me thinking of the slender naked girl I had seen on the bed and of the look in her eyes at the moment when she came up out of sleep and her eyes met mine.

"I knew her name and address and so one day I grew bold and wrote her a long letter. You must understand that by this time I felt I had become quite a sensible fellow and so I tried to write in a sensible way.

"I remember I was sitting in the writing-room of a small hotel in an Indiana town when I did it. The desk where I sat was by a window near the town's Main Street and, as it was evening, people were going along the street to their houses, I suppose going home to the evening meal.

"I don't deny I grew pretty romantic. As I sat there, feeling lonely and I suppose filled with self-pity, I looked up and saw a little drama acted out in a hallway across the street. There was a rather old tumble-down building with a stairway at the side running to an upper story where it was evident some one lived, as there were white curtains at the window.

"I sat looking across at the place, and I suppose I was dreaming of the long slender body of the girl on the bed upstairs in another house. It was evening and growing dusk, you understand, and just such a light as had fallen over us at the moment we looked into each other's eyes, at the moment when there was no one but just our two selves, before we had time to think and remember the others in that house, when I was coming out of a day-dream and she was coming out of the dreams of sleep, at the moment when we accepted each other and the complete and momentary loveliness of each other—well, you see, just such a light as I had stood in and she had lain in as one might lie on the soft waters of some southern sea, just such another light was now lying over the little bare writing-room of the foul little hotel in that town and across the street a woman came down the stairway and stood in just such another light.

"As it turned out she was also tall, like your mother, but I could not see what kind or color*of clothes she wore. There was some peculiarity of the light; an illusion was created. The devil! I wish I could tell of things that have happened to me without this eternal business of having everything I say seem a little strange and uncanny. One walks in a wood at evening, let us say, Jane, and one has queer fascinating illusions. The light, the shadows cast by trees, the open spaces between trees—these things create the illusions. Often the trees seem to beckon to one. Old sturdy trees look wise and you think they are going to tell you some great secret, but they don't. One gets into a forest of young birches. What naked girlish things, running and running, free, free. Once I was in such a wood with a girl. We were up to something. Well, it had gone no further than that we had a tremendous feeling for each other at the moment. We had kissed and I remember that twice I had stopped in the half-darkness and had touched her face with my fingers— tenderly and softly, you know. She was a little dumb shy girl I had picked up on the streets of an Indiana town, a kind of free immoral little thing, such as sometimes pop up in such towns. I mean she was free with men in a kind of queer shy way. I had picked her up on the street and then, when we got out there in the wood, we both felt the strangeness of things and the strangeness of being with each other too.

"There we were, you see. We were about to— I don't exactly know what we were up to. We were standing and looking at each other.

"And then we both looked suddenly up and there, in the path before us, was a very dignified and beautiful old man. He was wearing a robe that was caught over his shoulders, in a swaggering kind of a way, and it was spread out behind him over the floor of the forest, between the trees.

"What a princely old man! What a kingly fellow, in fact! We both saw him, both stood looking at him with eyes filled with wonder, and he stood looking at us.

"I had to go forward and touch the thing with my hands before the illusion our minds had created could be dispelled. The kingly old man was just a half-decayed old stump and the robe he wore was just the purple*night shadows falling down on the floor of the forest, but our having seen the thing together made everything different between the shy little town girl and myself. What we had perhaps both intended doing couldn't be done in the spirit in which we had approached it. I mustn't try to tell you of that now. I mustn't get too much off the track.

"What I am thinking is merely that such things

happen. I am talking of another time and place, you see. On that other evening, as I sat in the hotel writing-room, there was just such another light, and across the street a girl, or a woman, was coming down a stairway. I had the illusion that she was nude like a young birch tree and that she was coming toward me. Her face made a grayish wavering shadow-like spot in the hallway and she was evidently waiting for some one as she kept thrusting her head out and looking up and down the street.

"I became a fool again. That's the story, I dare say. As I sat looking and leaning forward, trying to see deeper and deeper into the evening light, a man came hurrying along the street and stopped at the stairway. He was tall like herself and when he stopped I remember that he took off his hat and stepped into the darkness holding it in his hand. There was probably something stealthy and covered-up about the love affair between the two people as the man also put his head out of the stairway and looked long and carefully up and down the street before taking the woman into his arms. Perhaps she was some other man's wife. Anyway they stepped back a little into a greater darkness and, I thought, took each other quite completely. How much I saw and how much I imagined I'll of course never know. At any rate the two grayish white faces seemed to float and then merge and become one grayish white spot.

"A violent tremor ran through my body. There, it seemed to me, but a few hundred feet from where I sat, now almost in complete darkness, was love finding glorious expression. Lips clung to lips, two warm bodies pressed close to each other, something altogether glorious and lovely in life, that I, by running about in the evening with the poor little girls of the town, and by trying to induce them to go with me into the fields to serve only my animal hunger—well, you see, there was a thing one might find in life that I had not found and that at the moment I thought I had failed to find because, at a great crisis, I had not found courage to go persistently toward it."*

IV

"And so you see I lighted a lamp in the writing-room of that hotel and forgot my supper and sat there and wrote pages and pages to the woman, and grew foolish too and confessed a lie, that I was ashamed of the thing that had happened between us some months before, and that I had only done it, that is to say, that I had only run into the room to her that second time, because I was a fool and a lot of other unspeakable nonsense."

John Webster jumped to his feet and started to walk nervously about the room, but now his daughter became something more than a passive listener to his tale. He had walked to where the Virgin stood between the burning candles and was moving back toward the door, that led into the hallway and down stairs, when she sprang up and running to him impulsively threw her arms about his neck. She began to sob and buried her face on his shoulder. "I love you," she said. "I don't care what's happened, I love you."

V

AND so there was John Webster in his house and he had succeeded, at least for the moment, in breaking through the wall that had separated him from his daughter. After her outburst they went and sat together on the bed, with his arm about her and her head on his shoulder. Years afterward, sometimes, when he was with a friend and was in a certain mood, John Webster occasionally spoke of that moment as having been the most important and lovely of his whole life. In a way his daughter had given herself to him as he had given himself to her. There had been a kind of marriage, that he realized. "I have been a father as well as a lover. Perhaps the two things cannot be differentiated. I have been one father who has not been afraid to realize the loveliness of his daughter's flesh and to fill my senses with the fragrance of it," was what he said.

As it turned out he might have sat thus, talking with his daughter, for another half-hour and then left the house to go away with Natalie, without any more drama, but that his wife, lying on the bed in the next room, heard her daughter's cry of love and it must have stirred something deeply buried away in her. She got silently off the bed and going to the door opened it softly. Then she stood leaning against the door-frame and listening as her husband talked. There was a look of hard terror in her eyes. Perhaps she wanted at that moment to kill the man who had for so long a time been her husband and did not do so only because the long years of inaction and submission into life had made it impossible for her to lift an arm to strike.

At any rate she stood in silence and one might have thought that she would at any moment fall to the floor, but she didn't. She waited and John Webster kept on talking. Now he was telling his daughter with a kind of devilish attention to details all the story of their marriage.

What had happened, at least in the man's version of the affair, was that, after having written one letter he could not stop and wrote another on the same evening and two more on the following day.

He kept on writing letters and what he himself thought was that the letter writing had created within him a kind of furious passion of lying that, once started, couldn't be stopped. "I began something that has been going on in me all these years," he explained. "It is a trick one practises, this lying to oneself about oneself." It was evident his daughter did not follow him, although she tried. He was talking now of something she had not experienced, could not have experienced, that is to say, the hypnotic power of words. Already she had read books and had been tricked by words, but there was in her no realization of what had already been done to her. She was a young girl and as, often enough, there was nothing in the life about her that seemed exciting or interesting she was thankful for the life of words and books. It was true they left one quite blank, went out of the mind leaving no trace. Well, they were created out of a kind of dream world. One had to have lived, to have experienced much of life, before one could come to the realization that just beneath the surface of ordinary everyday life there was deep and moving drama always going on. Few come to realization of the poetry of the actual.*

It was evident her father had come to some such realization. Now he was talking. He was opening doors for her. It was like travelling in an old town one had thought one knew, with a marvellously inspired guide. One went in and out of old houses, seeing things as they had never been seen before. All the things of everyday life, a picture on the wall, an old chair sitting by a table, the table itself at which a man one had always known, sits*smoking a pipe.

By some miracle all these things were now being invested with new life and significance.

The painter Van Gogh, who it is said killed himself in a fit of desperation because he could not gather within the limits of his canvas all the wonder and glory of the sun shining in the sky, once painted a canvas. An old chair set in an empty room.* When Jane Webster grew to be a woman and had got her own understanding of life she once saw the canvas hanging in a gallery in the city of New York. There was a strange wonder of life to be got from looking at the painting of an ordinary, roughly made chair

148

that had perhaps been owned by some peasant of France, some peasant at whose house the painter had perhaps stopped for an hour on a summer day.

It must have been a day when he was very much alive and very conscious of all the life of the house in which he sat and so he painted the chair and channeled into the painting all of the emotional reactions within himself to the people in that particular house and in many other houses he had visited.

Jane Webster was in the room with her father and his arm was about her and he was talking of something she couldn't understand and yet she did understand too. Now he was again a young man and was feeling the loneliness and uncertainty of young manhood as she had already sometimes felt the loneliness and uncertainty of her own young womanhood. Like her father she must begin to try to understand things a little. Now he was an honest man, he was talking to her honestly. There was wonder in that alone.

In his young manhood he went about towns, getting in with girls, doing with girls a thing she had heard whispers about. That made him feel unclean. He did not feel deeply enough the thing he did with the poor little girls. His body had made love to women, but he had not. That her father knew, but she did not yet know. There was much she did not know.

Her father, then a young man, had begun writing letters to a woman into whose presence he once came quite nude as he had appeared before her but a short time before. He was trying to explain how his mind, feeling about, had alighted upon the figure of a certain woman as one towards whom love might be directed.

He sat in a room in a hotel and wrote the word "love" in black ink on a white sheet of paper. Then he went out to walk in the quiet night streets of the town. She got the picture of him now quite clearly. The strangeness of his being so much older than herself and of his being her father had gone away. He was a man and she was a woman. She wanted to quiet the clamoring voices within him, to fill the blank empty spaces. She pressed her body more closely against his.

His voice kept explaining things. There was a passion for explanation in him.

As he sat in the hotel he had written certain words on paper and putting the paper into an envelope had sent it away to a woman living in a distant place. Then he walked and walked and thought of more words and going back to the hotel wrote them out on other pieces of paper.

A thing was created within him it was hard to explain, that he had not understood himself. One walked under the stars and in quiet streets of towns under trees and sometimes, on summer evenings, heard voices in the darkness. People, men and women, were sitting in the darkness on the porches of houses. There was an illusion created. One sensed in the darkness somewhere a deep quiet splendor*of life and ran toward it. There was a

150

kind of desperate eagerness. In the sky the stars shone more splendidly because of one's thoughts. There was a little wind and it was like the hand of a lover touching the cheeks, playing in one's hair. There was something lovely in life one must find. When one was young one could not stand still, but must go toward it. The writing of the letters was an effort to go toward the thing. It was an effort to find footing in the darkness on strange winding roads.

And so John Webster had, by his letter writing, done a strange and false thing to himself and to the woman who was later to be his wife. He had created a world of unrealities. Would he and the woman be able to live together in that world?*

VI

In the semi-darkness of the room, as the man talked to his daughter trying to make her understand an intangible thing, the woman who had been his wife for so many years and out of whose body had come the younger woman who now sat close to her husband, began also to try to understand. After a time, and being unable to stand longer, she managed, without attracting the attention of the others, to slip to the floor. She let her back slide down along the frame of the door and her legs turned sideways under her heavy body. In the position into which she had got she was uncomfortable and her knees hurt, but she did not mind. There was in fact a kind of satisfaction to be got from physical discomfort.

One had lived for so many years in a world that was now and before one's very eyes being destroyed. There was something wicked and ungodly in this business of defining life too sharply. Certain things should not be spoken of. One moved dimly through a dim world not asking too many questions. If there was death in silence, then one accepted death. What was the use of denial? One's body got old and heavy. When one sat on the floor the knees hurt. There was something unbearable in this notion that a man, with whom one had lived so many years of life and whom one had accepted quite definitely as a part of the machinery of life, should suddenly become something else, should become this terrible questioner, this raker-up of forgotten things.

If one lived behind a wall one preferred life behind the wall. Behind the wall the light was dim and did not hurt the eyes. Memories were shut out. The sounds of life grew faint and indistinct in the distance. There was something barbaric and savage in all this business of breaking down walls, making cracks and gaps in the wall of life.

There was a struggle going on within the woman, Mary Webster, also. A queer sort of new life came and went in her eyes. Had a fourth person at that moment come into the room he might have been more conscious of her than of the others.

There was something terrible in the way her husband John Webster had set the stage for the battle that was now to go on within her. The man was after all a dramatist. The business of buying the picture of the Virgin and the candles, the making of this little stage upon which a drama was to be played out; there was an unconscious art expression in all this.

Perhaps he had outwardly intended nothing of the sort, but with what devilish certainty he had worked. The woman now sat in a half-darkness on the floor. Between her and the burning candles was the bed on which the two others sat, one talking, the other listening. All the floor of the room, near where she sat was in heavy black shadows. She had put one hand out against the door-frame to help support herself.

The candles on their high place flickered as they burned. The light fell only on her shoulders, her head, and her upraised arm and hand.

She was almost submerged in a sea of darkness. Now and then, from sheer weariness her head fell forward and there was an effect of sinking completely into the sea.

Still her arm was upraised and her head came back again to the surface of the sea. There was a slight rocking movement to her body. She was like an old boat, half water-logged, lying in the sea. Little fluttering waves of light seemed playing over her heavy white upraised face.

Breathing was somewhat difficult. Thinking was somewhat difficult. One had gone along for years without thinking. It was better to lie quietly in a sea of silence. The world was quite right in excommunicating those who disturbed the sea of silence. Mary Webster's body quivered a little. One might kill, but had not the strength to kill, did not know how to kill. Killing was a business one had to learn too.

It was unbearable, but one had at times to think. Things happened. A woman married a man and then found, quite suddenly, she had not married him. The world was getting strange unacceptable notions about marriage. Daughters should not be told such things as her husband was now telling their daughter. Could the mind of a young virginal girl be raped, by her own father, into consciousness of unspeakable things in life? If such things were permitted what would become of all decent orderly living of lives? Virginal girls should find out nothing about life until the time came to live the things they must, being women, finally accept.

In every human body there is a great well of silent thinking always going on. Outwardly certain words are said, but there are other words being said at the same time down in the deep hidden places. There is a deposit of thoughts, of unexpressed emotions. How many things thrown down into the deep well, hidden away in the deep well!

There is a heavy iron lid clamped over the mouth of the well. When the lid is safely in place one gets on all right. One goes about saying words, eating food, meeting people, conducting affairs, accumulating money, wearing clothes, one lives an ordered life.

Sometimes at night, in dreams, the lid trembles, but no one knows about that.

Why should there be those who desire to tear the lids off the wells, to break through the walls? Things had better be left as they are. Those who disturb the heavy iron lids should be killed.

The heavy iron lid over the deep well that was within the body of Mary Webster was trembling violently. It danced up and down. The dancing light from the candles was like the little playful waves on the surface of a calm sea. It met in her eyes another kind of dancing light.

On the bed John Webster talked freely and easily. If he had set the stage he had also given himself the talking rôle in the drama that was to be played out upon it. His own thought had been that everything that happened on that evening was directed toward his daughter. He had even dared to think he might be able to re-channel her life. Her young life was like a river that was still small and made but a slight murmuring sound as it ran through quiet fields. One might still step across the stream that was later, and when it had taken other streams into itself, to become a river. One might venture to throw a log across the stream, to start it off in a quite different direction. The whole thing was a daring, a quite reckless thing to do, but one could not quite escape some such action.

Now he had dismissed from his mind the other woman, his former wife, Mary Webster. He had thought when she went out of the bedroom she had finally walked off the stage. There had been satisfaction in seeing her go. He had really, in all their life together, never made a contact with her. When he thought her gone from the field of his own life he felt relieved.* One could breathe more deeply, talk more freely.

He thought of her as having gone off the stage, but she had come back. He still had her to deal with too.

In Mary Webster's mind memories were awakening. Her husband was telling the story of his marriage, but she did not hear his words. A story began to tell itself within her, beginning far back on a day in her own young womanhood.

She had heard the cry of love for a man come out of her daughter's throat and the cry had stirred something within her so deeply that she had come back into the room where her husband and daughter sat together on the bed. Once there had been that same cry within another young woman, but for some reason it had never got itself out, past her lips. At the moment when it might have come from her, at that moment long ago when she lay naked on a bed and looked into the eyes of a young naked man something, a thing people called shame, had come between her and the getting of that glad cry past her lips.

Her mind now wearily went back over the details of the scene. An old railroad journey was retravelled.

Things were tangled. First she lived in one place and then, as though pushed into the act by a hand she could not see, she went on a visit to another place.

The journey there was taken in the middle of the night and, as there were no sleeping cars on the train, she had to sit in a day-coach through several hours of darkness.

Outside the car window there was darkness, broken now and then when the train stopped for a few minutes at some town in Western Illinois or Southern Wisconsin. There was a station build-

ing with a lamp fastened to the outer wall and sometimes but a solitary man, bundled in a coat and perhaps pushing a truck piled with trunks and boxes
along a station platform.   At some of the towns
people got aboard the train and at others people got
off and went away into the darkness.

An old woman who carried a basket in which
there was a black and white cat came to sit in the
seat with her and after she had got off at one of the
stations an old man took her place.

The old man did not look at her, but kept muttering words she could not catch.   He had a ragged
gray*moustache that hung down over his shrunken
lips and he continually stroked it with a bony old
hand.   The words he said in an undertone were
muttered behind the hand.

The young woman of that railroad journey, taken
long ago, had, after a time, fallen into a half-wak-
ing, half-sleeping state.   Her mind had run ahead
of her body to her journey's end.   A girl she had
known at school had invited her for a visit and there
had been several letters written back and forth.
Two young men would be in the house all during
the time of the visit.

One of the young men she had already seen.   He
was her friend's brother and had once come on a
visit to the school where the two girls were stu-
dents.

What would the other young man be like?   It
was curious how many times she had already asked
herself that question.   Now her mind was making
fanciful pictures of him.

The train ran through a country of low hills. Dawn was coming. It would be a day of gray cold clouds. Snow threatened. The muttering old man of the gray*moustache and the bony hand had got off the train.

The half-awake eyes of the tall slender young woman looked out over low hills and long stretches of flat land. The train crossed a bridge over a river. She slipped into sleep and was jerked out again by the starting or stopping of the train. Across a distant field a young man was walking in the gray*morning light.

Had she dreamed there was a young man going across a field beside the train or had she actually seen such a man? In what way was he connected with the young man she was to meet at her journey's end?

It was a little absurd to think the young man in the field could be of flesh and blood. He walked at the same pace the train was going stepping lightly over fences, going swiftly through the streets of towns, passing like a shadow through strips of dark woodland.

When the train stopped he also stopped and stood looking at her and smiling. One almost felt he could*go into one's body and come out smiling thus. The idea was strangely sweet too. Now he walked for a long time on the surface of the waters of a river alongside which the train was running.

And all the time he looked into her eyes, darkly, when the train passed through a forest and it was dark inside the train, with a smile in his eyes when they came out again into the open country. There was something in his eyes that invited, called to her. Her body grew warm and she stirred uneasily in the car seat.

The trainmen*had built a fire in a stove at the end of the car and all the doors and windows were closed. Evidently it was not going to be such a cold day after all. It was unbearably hot in the car.

She got out of her seat and, clutching at the edges of other seats, made her way to the end of the car where she opened a door and stood for a time looking at the flying landscape.

The train came to the station where she was to get off and there, on the station platform, was her girl friend, come to the station on the odd chance she would come on that train.

And then she had gone with her friend into the strange house and her friend's mother had insisted she go to bed and sleep until evening. The two women kept asking how it had happened she had come on that train and as she could not explain she became a little embarrassed. It was true there was another and faster train she might have taken and had the entire ride in the day-time.

There had just been a kind of feverish desire to get out of her own town and her mother's house. She had been unable to explain that to her own people. One couldn't tell one's mother and father she just wanted to get out. In her own home there had been a confusion of questions about the whole matter. Well, there she was, being driven into a corner and asked questions that couldn't be answered. She had a hope that her girl friend would understand and kept hopefully saying to her what she had said over and over rather senselessly at home. "I just wanted to do it. I don't know, I just wanted to do it."

In the strange house she had got into bed to sleep, glad to escape the annoying question. When she awoke they would have forgotten the whole matter. Her friend had come into the room with her and she wanted to dismiss her quickly, to be alone for a time. "I'll not unpack my bag now. I think I'll just undress and crawl in between the sheets. It's going to be warm anyway," she explained. It was absurd. Well she had looked forward to something quite different on her arrival, laughter, young men standing about and looking a little self-conscious. Now she only felt uncomfortable. Why did people keep asking why she had got up at midnight and taken a slow train instead of waiting until morning? One wanted sometimes just to be a fool about little things, and not to have to give explanations. When her friend went out of the room she threw off all her clothes and got quickly into bed and closed her eyes. It was another foolish notion she had, her wanting to be naked. Had she not taken the slow uncomfortable train she would not have had the fancy about the young man walking beside the train in the fields, through the streets of towns, through forests.

It was good to be naked sometimes. There was the feel of things against one's skin. If one could only have the joyful feeling of that more often. One could sink into a clean bed, sometimes, when one was tired and sleepy and it was like getting into the firm warm arms of some one who could love and understand one's foolish impulses.

The young woman in the bed slept and in her sleep was again being carried swiftly along through the darkness. The woman with the cat and the old man who muttered words did not appear again, but many other people came and went through her dream-world. There was a swift tangled march of strange events. She went forward, always forward toward something she wanted. Now it approached. A great eagerness took possession of her.

It was strange that she wore no clothes. The young man who walked so swiftly through fields had reappeared, but she had not noticed before that he also did not wear clothes.

The world had grown dark. There was a dusky darkness.

And now the young man had stopped going swiftly forward and like herself was silent. They both hung suspended in a sea of silence. He was standing and looking directly into her eyes. He could go within her and come out again. The thought was infinitely sweet.

She lay in a soft warm darkness and her flesh was

hot, too hot. "Some one has foolishly built a fire and has forgotten to open the doors and windows," she thought vaguely.

The young man, who was now so close to her, who was standing silently so close to her and looking directly into her eyes, could make everything all right. His hands were within a few inches of her body. In a moment they would touch, bring cool peace into her body, into herself too.

There was a sweet peace to be got by looking directly into the young man's eyes. They were glowing in the darkness like little pools into which one could cast oneself. A final and infinite peace and joy could be got by casting oneself into the pools.

Could one stay thus, lying quietly in the soft warm dark pools? One had got into a secret place, behind a high wall. Outside voices cried—"Shame! Shame!" When one listened to the voices the pools became foul loathsome places. Should one listen to the voices or should one close the ears, close the eyes? The voices beyond the wall became louder and louder—crying, "Shame! Be ashamed!" To listen to the voices brought death. Did closing one's ears to the voices bring death too?*

VII

JOHN WEBSTER was telling a story. There was a thing he himself wanted to understand. Wanting to understand things was a new passion, come to him. What a world he had lived in always and how little he had wanted to understand it. Children were being born in towns and on farms. They grew up to be men and women. Some of them went to colleges, others, after a few years in the town or country schools, got out into life, married perhaps, got jobs in factories or shops, went to church on Sundays or to a ball game, became parents of children.

People everywhere told things,* talked of things they thought interested them, but no one told truths. At school there was no attention paid to truth. What a tangle of other and unimportant things. "Two and two make four. If a merchant sell three oranges and two apples to a man and oranges are to be sold at twenty-four cents per dozen and apples at sixteen, how much does the man owe the merchant?"

An important matter indeed. Where is the fellow going with the three oranges and two apples? He is a small man in brown boots and has his cap stuck on the side of his head. There is a peculiar smile playing around his mouth. The sleeve of his coat is torn. What did that? The cuss is singing a song under his breath. Listen:

> "Diddle de di do,
> Diddle de di do,
> Chinaberries grow on a Chinaberry tree.
> Diddle de di do."

What in the name of the bearded men, who came into the queen's bed-chamber when the king of Rome was born, does he mean by that? What is a Chinaberry tree?

John Webster talked to his daughter, sat with his arm about her talking, and back of him, and unseen, his wife struggled and fought to put back into its place the iron lid one should always keep tightly clamped down on the opening of the well of unexpressed thoughts within oneself.

There was a man who had come naked into her naked presence in the dusk of the late afternoon of a day long ago. He had come in to her and had done a thing to her. There had been a rape of the unconscious self. That had been in time forgotten or forgiven, but now he was doing it again. He was talking now. Of what was he talking? Were there not things of which one never talked? For what purpose the deep well within oneself except that it be a place into which one could put the things that must not be talked about?

Now John Webster was trying to tell the whole

story of his attempt at love-making with the woman he had married.

The writing of letters containing the word "love," had come to something. After a time, and when he had sent off several such letters written in the hotel writing-rooms, and just when he was beginning to think he would never get an answer to one of them and might as well give the whole matter up, an answer had come. Then there had burst from him a flood of letters.

He was still then going about from town to town trying to sell washing machines to merchants, but that only took a part of each day. There was left the late afternoons, mornings when he arose early and sometimes went for a walk along the streets of one of the towns before breakfast, the long evenings and the Sundays.

He was full of unaccountable energy all through that time. It must have been because he was in love. If one were not in love one could not feel so alive. In the early mornings, and in the evenings as he walked about, looking at houses and people, every one suddenly seemed close to him. Men and women came out of houses and went along the streets, factory whistles blew, men and boys went in and out at the doors of factories.

He was standing by a tree on a strange street of a strange town in the evening. In a nearby house a child cried and a woman's voice talked to it in low tones. His fingers gripped the bark of the tree. He wanted to run into·the house where the child was crying, to take the child out of its mother's arms and quiet it, to kiss the mother perhaps. What a thing it would be if he could only go along a street shaking men by the hand, putting his arms about the shoulders of young girls.

He had extravagant fancies. There might be a world in which there were new and marvellous cities. He went along imagining such cities. For one thing the doors to all the houses were wide open. Everything was clean and neat. The sills to the doors of the houses had been washed. He walked into one of the houses. Well, the people had gone out, but on the chance some such fellow as himself would wander in they had set out a little feast on a table in one of the rooms downstairs. There was a loaf of white bread with a carving knife lying beside it so that one could cut off slices, cold meats, little squares of cheese, a decanter of wine.

He sat alone at the table to eat, feeling very happy, and after his hunger had been satisfied carefully brushed away the crumbs and fixed everything nicely. Some other fellow might come along later and wander into the same house.

The fancies young Webster had during that period of his life filled him with delight. Sometimes he stopped in his night walks along dark residence streets and stood looking up at the sky and laughing.

There he was in a world of fancies, in a place of dreams. His mind plunged him back into the house he had visited in his dream-world. What curiosity there was in him in regard to the people who lived there. It was night, but the place was lighted.

There were little lamps one could pick up and carry about. There was a city, wherein each house was a feasting place and this was one of the houses and in its sweet depths things other than the belly could be fed.

One went through the house feeding all the senses. The walls had been painted with strong colors*that had now faded and become soft and mellow with age. The time had passed in America when people continually built new houses. They built houses strongly and then stayed in them, beautified them slowly and with a sure touch. One would perhaps rather be in such a house in the day-time when the owners were at home, but it was fine to be there alone at night too.

The lamp held above one's head threw dancing shadows on the walls. One went up a stairway into bedrooms, wandered in halls, came down the stairs again and putting the lamp back into its place passed out at the open front door.

How sweet to linger on the front steps for a moment, having more dreams. What of the people who lived in the house? In one of the bedrooms upstairs he had fancied he knew that a young woman slept. Had she been in the bed and asleep and had he walked in on her, what would have happened?

Might there be in the world, well, one might as well say in some world of the fancy—perhaps it would take too much time for an actual people to create such a world—but might there not be a people, in the world of one's fancy, a people who had really developed the senses, people who really smelled, saw, tasted, felt things with their fingers, heard things with their ears? One could dream of such a world. It was early evening and for several hours one did not have to go back to the little dirty town hotel.

Some day there might be a world inhabited by people who lived. There would be, then, an end of continual mouthings about death. People would take life up firmly like a filled cup and carry it until the time came to throw it away over the shoulder with a gesture. They would realize that wine was made to drink, food to eat and nourish the body, the ears to hear all manner of sounds, the eyes to see things.

Within the bodies of such people what unknown senses might there not be developed? Well, it might very well be that a young woman,* such as John Webster was trying to fancify into existence, that on such evenings such a young woman* might be lying quietly in a bed in an upper chamber of one of the houses along the dark street. One went in at the open door of the house and taking up the lamp went to her. One could fancy the lamp itself as a thing of beauty too. There was a small ring-like arrangement through which one slipped the finger. One wore the lamp like a ring on the finger. The little flame of it was like a jewel shining in the darkness.

One went up the stairs and softly into the room where the woman was lying on the bed. One held the lamp above one's head. Its light shone into

169

one's eyes and into the eyes of the woman. There was a long slow time when the two just remained so, looking at each other.*

There was a question being asked. "Are you for me? Am I for you?" People had developed a new sense, many new senses. People saw with their eyes, smelled with their nostrils, heard with their ears. The deeper-lying, buried-away senses of the body had been developed too. Now people could accept or dismiss one another with a gesture. There was no more slow starvation of men and women. Long lives did not have to be lived during which one knew, and then but faintly, a few half-golden moments.

There was something about all this having fancies closely connected with his marriage and with his life since his marriage. He was trying to make that clear to his daughter but it was difficult.

There had been that moment once, when he had gone into the upper room of a house and had found a woman lying before him. There had been a question come suddenly and unexpectedly into his own eyes and it had found a quick eager answer in hers.

And then—the devil, it was hard to get things straight! In some way a lie had been told. By whom? There had been a poison he and the woman had breathed together. Who had blown the cloud of poison vapor*into the air of that upper bed-chamber?

The moment had kept coming back into the mind of the young man. He walked in streets of strange towns having thoughts of coming into the upper bed-chamber of a new kind of womanhood.

Then later he went to the hotel and sat for hours writing letters. To be sure he did not write out the fancies he had been having. O, had he but had the courage to do that! Had he but known enough to do that!

What he did was to write the word "love," over and over rather stupidly. "I went walking and I thought of you and I loved you so. I saw a house I liked and I thought of you and me living in it as man and wife. I am sorry I was so stupid and blundering when I saw you that other time. Give me another chance and I will prove my 'love' to you."

What a betrayal! It was John Webster himself who had, in the end, poisoned the wells of truth at which he and the woman would have to drink as they went along the road toward happiness.

He hadn't been thinking of her at all. He had been thinking of the strange mysterious woman lying in the upper bed-chamber in the city of the land of his fancy.

Everything got started wrong and then nothing could be set straight again. One day a letter came from her and then, after writing a great many other letters, he went to her town to see her.

There was a time of embarrassment and then the past was apparently forgotten. They went to walk together under the trees in a strange town. Later he wrote more letters and came to see her again. One night he asked her to marry him.

The very devil! He didn't even take her into his arms when he asked her. There was a kind of fear involved in the whole matter. "I'd better not after what happened before. I'll wait until we're married. Things will be different then." One had a notion. It was that after marriage one became something quite different from what one had been before and that the beloved one also became something quite different.

And so he had managed to get married, having that notion, and he and the woman had set out together upon a wedding trip.

John Webster held his daughter's body closely against his own and trembled a little. "I had some notion in my head that I had better go slow," he said. "You see, I had already frightened her once. 'We'll go slow here,' I kept saying to myself; 'well, she doesn't know much about life, I'd better go pretty slow.'"

The memory of the moment of his marriage stirred John Webster profoundly.

The bride was coming down a stairway. Strange people stood about. All the time, down inside the strange people, down inside all people everywhere, there was thinking going on of which no one seemed aware.

"Now you look at me, Jane. I'm your father. I was that way. All these years, while I've been your father, I've been just like that.

"Something happened to me. A lid was jerked off something somewhere in me.* Now, you see, I stand, as though on a high hill and look down into a valley where all my former life has been lived. Quite suddenly, you understand, I know all the thoughts I've been having all of my life.

"You'll hear it said. Well, you'll read it in books and stories people write about death. 'At the moment of death he looked back and saw all his life spread out before him.' That's what you'll read.

"Ha! That's all right, but what about life? What about the moment, when, having been dead, one comes back into life?"

John Webster had got himself excited again. He took his arm from about his daughter's shoulder and rubbed his hands together. A slight shivering sensation ran through his body and through the body of his daughter. She did not understand what he was saying, but in a queer sense that did not matter. They were, at the moment deeply in accord. This having one's whole being suddenly become alive, after years of a kind of partial death, was a strain. One had to get a kind of new balance to the body and mind. One felt very young and strong and then suddenly old and tired. Now one was carrying his life forward as one might carry a filled cup through a crowded street. All the time one had to remember, to keep in mind, that there must be a certain relaxation to the body. One must give and swing with things a little. That must always be borne in mind. If one became rigid and tense at any time, except at the moment when one cast one's body into the body of one's beloved, one's foot stumbled or one knocked against things and the filled cup one carried was emptied with an awkward gesture.

Strange thoughts kept coming into the mind of the man as he sat on the bed with his daughter trying to get himself in hand. One might very easily become one of the kind of people one saw everywhere about, one of the kind of people whose empty bodies went walking everywhere in towns and cities and on farms, "one of the kind of people whose life is an empty cup," he thought and then a more majestic thought came and steadied him. There was something he had heard or read about sometime. What was it? "Arouse not up or awaken my love 'til he please," a voice within him said.

Again he began the telling of the story of his marriage.

"We went off on our wedding trip to a farmhouse in Kentucky, went there in the sleeping car of a train at night. I kept thinking about going slow with her, kept telling myself all the time I'd better go slow so that night she slept in a lower berth while I crept into the one above.* We were going on a visit to a farm owned by her uncle, by her father's brother, and we got to the town, where we were to get off the train, before breakfast in the morning.

"Her uncle was waiting with a carriage at the

station and we drove off at once to this place in the country where we were to visit."

John Webster told with great attention to details the story of the arrival of the two people at the little town. He had slept but little during the night and was very aware of everything going on about him. There was a row of wooden store buildings that led up from the station and, within a few hundred yards, it became a residence street and then a country road. A man in his shirt sleeves walked along the sidewalk on one side the street. He was smoking a pipe, but as the carriage passed he took the pipe out of his mouth and laughed. He called to another man who stood before the open door of a store on the opposite side of the street. What strange words he was saying. What did they mean? "Make it fancy, Eddie," he called.

The carriage containing the three people drove quickly along. John Webster had not slept during the night and there was a kind of straining at something within him. He was all alive, eager. Her uncle on the front seat was a large man, like her father, but living as he did out of doors had made the skin of his face brown. He also had a gray moustache. Could one get acquainted with him? Would one ever be able to say intimate confidential things to him?

For that matter would one ever be able to say intimate confidential things to the woman one had married? The truth was that all night his body had been aching with anticipation of a coming love-mak-

ing. How odd that one did not speak of such matters when one had married women out of respectable
families in respectable Illinois manufacturing towns.*
At the wedding every one must have known. That
was no doubt what the young married men and
women were smiling and laughing about, behind the
walls, as it were.

There were two horses hitched to the carriage
and they went soberly and steadily along. Now the
woman who had become John Webster's bride, was
sitting up, very straight and tall on the seat beside
him and she had her hands folded in her lap. They
were nearing the edge of town and a boy came out
at the front door of a house and stood on a little
porch staring at them with blank questioning eyes.
There was a large dog asleep beneath a cherry tree
beside another house a little further along. He
let the carriage get almost past before he moved.
John Webster watched the dog. "Shall I get up
from this comfortable place and make a fuss about
that carriage or shall I not?" the dog seemed to be
asking himself. Then he sprang up and racing
madly along the road began barking at the horses.
The man on the front seat struck at him with the
whip. "I suppose he made up his mind he had to
do it, that it was the proper thing to do," John Webster said. His bride and her uncle both looked at
him with questioning eyes. "Eh, what's that?
What'd you say?" the uncle asked, but got no answer. John Webster felt suddenly embarrassed.
"I was only speaking of the dog," he said presently.

176

One had to make some kind of explanation. The rest of the ride was taken in silence.

It was late on that same afternoon that the thing to which he had been looking forward with so much hope and doubt came to a kind of consummation.

Her uncle's farmhouse, a large comfortable white frame building, stood on the bank of a river in a narrow green valley and hills rose up before and behind it. In the afternoon young Webster and his bride walked past the barn, back of the house, and got into a lane that ran beside an orchard. Then they crawled over a fence and crossing a field got into a wood that led up the hillside. There was another meadow above and then another wood that covered the top of the hill quite completely.

It was a warm day and they tried to talk as they went along, but did not succeed very well. Now and then she looked at him shyly, as though to say, "The road we are thinking of taking in life is very dangerous. Are you quite sure you are a safe guide?"

Well he had felt her questioning and was in doubt about the answer to be made. It would have been better no doubt had the question been asked and answered long ago. When they came to a narrow path in the wood, he let her walk ahead and then he could look at her quite boldly. There was fear in him too. "Our self-consciousness is going to make us muddle everything," he thought. It was hard to remember whether he really had thought anything so definite at that time. He was afraid. Her back was very straight and once when she stooped to pass under the limb of an overhanging tree, her long slender body going down and up made a very lovely gesture. A lump came into his throat.*

He tried to keep his mind fixed on little things. There had been rain a day or two before and little mushrooms grew beside the path. In one spot there was a whole army of them, very graceful and with their 'caps touched with tender splashes of color. He picked one of them. How strangely pungent to the nostrils. He wanted to eat it, but she was frightened and protested. "Don't," she said. "It may be a poison one." For a moment it seemed they might, after all, get acquainted. She looked directly at him. It was odd. They had not yet called each other endearing names. They did not address each other by any name at all. "Don't eat it," she said. "All right, but isn't it tempting and lovely?" he answered. They looked at each other for a moment and then she blushed, after which they went on again along the path.

They had got out upon the hill where they could look back over the valley and she sat with her back against a tree. Spring had passed, but, as they walked through the wood, there had been, on all sides, a sense of new growth springing up. Little green, pale green things were just pushing their way up from among the dead brown leaves and out of the black ground and on trees and bushes there was a sense of new growth too. Were new leaves coming or had the old leaves but begun to stand up a little straighter and more firmly because they had been refreshed? It was a thing to think about too, when one was puzzled and had before one a question wanting answering that one could not answer.

They were on the hill now and as he lay at her feet he did not need to look at her, but could look down across the valley. She might be looking at him and having thoughts just as he was, but that was her own affair. One did well enough to have one's own thoughts, straighten out one's own matters.* The rain that had freshened everything had stirred up many new smells in the wood. How fortunate there was no wind. The smells were not blown away, but were lying low, like a soft blanket over everything. The ground had a fragrance of its own and with it was blended the fragrance of decaying leaves and of animals too. There was a path along the top of the hill along which sheep sometimes went. Little piles of sheep-droppings were lying in the hard path back of the tree where she sat. He did not turn to look, but knew they were there. The sheep-droppings were like marbles. It was good to feel that within the compass of his love of smells he could include all life, even the excretions of life. Somewhere in the wood there was a kind of flowering tree. It couldn't be far away. The fragrance from it mingled with all the other smells floating over the hillside. The trees were calling to the bees and insects who were answering with mad eagerness. They flew swiftly along, in the air over John Webster's head, over her head too. One put off other things to play

179

with thoughts. One pitched little thoughts into the air idly, like boys at play, pitched and then caught them again. After a while, when the proper time came, there would be a crisis come into the lives of John Webster and the woman he had married, but now one played with thoughts. One pitched the thoughts into the air and caught them again.

People went about knowing the fragrance of flowers and a few other things, spices and the like, they had been told by the poets were fragrant. Could walls be erected about smells too? Was there not a Frenchman once who wrote a poem regarding the fragrance of the armpits of women? Was that something he had heard talked about among the young men at school or was it just a fool idea that had come into his own head?

The thing was to get the sense of the fragrance of all things, of earth, plants, peoples, animals, insects, all together in the mind. One could weave a golden mantle to spread over the earth and over people. The strong animal smells, taken with the smell of pine trees and all such heavy odors,* would give the mantle strength to wear well. Then upon the basis of that strength one could turn one's fancy loose.* Now was the time for all the minor poets to come running. On the solid basis John Webster's fancy had built, they could weave all manner of designs, using all the smells their less sturdy nostrils dare receive, the smell of violets growing beside woodland paths, of little fragile mushrooms, of honey dripping from the sacks under the bellies

180

of insects, of the hair of maidens fresh come from the bath.

After all John Webster, a man of the middle age, was sitting on a bed with his daughter talking of an experience of his youth. In spite of himself he was giving the tale of that experience a curiously perverted twist. No doubt he was lying to his daughter. Had that young man on the hillside, in the long ago, had the many and complicated feelings with which he was now endowing him?

Now and then he stopped talking and shook his head while a smile played across his face.

"How firmly now things were arranged between himself and his daughter. There was no doubt a miracle had been wrought."

He even fancied she knew he was lying, that he was throwing a certain mantle of romance over the experience of his young manhood, but he fancied she knew also that it was only by lying to the limit he could come at truth.*

Now one was back in fancy on the hillside again. There was an opening among the trees and through this one looked, seeing the whole valley below. There was a large town down the river somewhere, not the town where he and his bride had got off the train, but a much larger one with factories. Some people had come up the river in boats from the town and were preparing to have a picnic in a grove of trees, upstream and across the river from her uncle's house.

181

There were both men and women in the party and the women had on white dresses. It was charming to watch them moving in and out among the green trees and one of them came down to the river's edge and, putting one foot in a boat that was drawn up on the bank, and with the other on the bank itself, she leaned over to fill a pitcher with water. There was the woman* and her reflection in the water, seen faintly, even from this distance. There was a go· ing together and a coming apart. The two white figures opened and closed like a delicately tinted shell.

Young Webster on the hill had not looked at his bride and they were both silent, but he was becom· ing almost insanely excited. Was she thinking the thoughts he was thinking? Had her nature also opened itself, as had his?

It was becoming impossible to keep things straight in the mind. What was he thinking and what was she thinking and feeling? Far away in the wood across the river the white figures of women were moving about among trees.* The men of the picnic party, with their darker clothes could no longer be discerned. One no longer thought of them. The white-clad women's figures were being woven in and out among the sturdy upstanding trunks of the trees.

There was a woman on the hill behind him and she was his bride. Perhaps she was having just such thoughts as himself. That must be true. She was a woman and young and she would be afraid, but there came a time when fear must be put aside. One was a male and at the proper time went toward the female and took her. There was a kind of cruelty in nature and at the proper time that cruelty became a part of one's manhood.

He closed his eyes and rolling over to his belly got to his hands and knees.

If one stayed longer lying quietly at her feet there would be a kind of insanity. Already there was too much anarchy within. "At the moment of death all of life passes before a man." What a silly notion. "What about the moment of the coming of life?"

He was on his knees like an animal, looking at the ground, not yet looking at her. With all the strength of his being he tried to tell his daughter of the meaning of that moment in his life.

"How shall I say how I felt? Perhaps I should have been a painter or a singer. My eyes were closed and within myself were all the sights, sounds, smells, feeling of the world of the valley into which I had been looking. Within myself I comprehended all things.

"Things came in flashes, in colors. First there were the yellows, the golden shining yellow things, not yet born. The yellows were little streaks of shining color buried down with the dark blues and blacks of the soil. The yellows were things not yet born, not yet come into the light. They were yellow because they were not yet green. Soon the yellows would combine with the dark colors in the earth and spring forth into a world of color.

There would be a sea of color, running in waves, splashing over everything. Spring would come, within the earth, within myself too."

Birds were flying in the air over a river, and young Webster, with his eyes closed, crouched before the woman, was himself the birds in the air, the air itself, and the fishes in the river below. It seemed to him now that if he were to open his eyes and look back, down into the valley, he could see, even from that great distance, the movements of the fins of fishes in the waters of the river far below.

Well he had better not open his eyes now. Once he had looked into a woman's eyes and she had come to him like a swimmer coming up out of the sea, but then something had happened to spoil everything. He crept toward her. Now she had begun to protest. "Don't," she said, "I'm afraid."

It would not do to stop now. There was a time came when one must not stop. He threw his arms out, took her protesting and crying into his arms.

VIII

"WHY must one commit rape, rape of the conscious, rape of the unconscious?"

John Webster sprang up from beside his daughter and then whirled quickly about. A word had come out of the body of his wife sitting unobserved on the floor behind him. "Don't," she said and then, after opening and closing her mouth twice, ineffectually, repeated the word. "Don't, don't," she said again. The words seemed to be forcing themselves through her lips. Her body lumped down there on the floor had become just a strangely misshapen bundle of flesh and bones.

She was pale, of a pasty paleness.

John Webster had jumped off the bed as a dog, lying asleep in the dust of a roadway, might have leaped out of the path of a rapidly moving vehicle.

The devil! His mind was jerked back into the present swiftly, violently. A moment before he had been with a young woman on a hillside above a wide sun-washed valley and had been making love to her. The love-making had not been a success. It had turned out badly. There had been a tall slender girl who had submitted her body to a man, but who had been all the time terribly frightened and

185

beset by a sense of guilt and shame. After the love-making she had cried, not with an excess of tenderness, but because she had felt unclean. They had walked down the hillside later and she had tried to tell him how she felt. Then he also had begun to feel mean and unclean.* Tears had come into his own eyes. He had thought she must be right. What she said almost every one said. After all man was not an animal. Man was a conscious thing trying to struggle upward out of animalism. He had tried to think everything out that same night as he, for the first time, lay in bed beside his wife, and he had come to certain conclusions. She was no doubt right in her belief that there were certain impulses in men that had better be subjected to the power of the will. If one just let oneself go one became no better than a beast.

He had tried hard to think everything out clearly. What she had wanted was that there be no love-making between them except for the purpose of breeding children. If one went about the business of bringing children into the world, making new citizens for the state and all that, then one could feel a certain dignity in love-making. She had tried to explain how humiliated and mean she had felt that day when he had come into her naked presence. For the first time they had talked of that. It had been made ten times, a thousand times worse because he had come the second time and the others had seen him. The clean moment of their relationship was denied with determined insistence. After that had happened she could not bear to remain in the company of her girl friend and, as for her friend's brother—well, how could she ever look into his face again? Whenever he looked at her he would be seeing her not properly clothed as she should be, but shamelessly naked and on a bed with a naked man holding her in his arms. She had been compelled to get out of the house, go home at once, and of course, when she got home, every one wondered what had happened that her visit had come to such an abrupt end. The trouble was that when her mother was questioning her, on the day after her arrival home, she suddenly burst into tears.

What they thought after that she did not know.* The truth was that she had begun to be afraid of every one's thoughts. When she went into her bedroom at night she was almost ashamed to look at her own body and had got into the habit of undressing in the darkness. Her mother was always dropping remarks. "Did your coming home so suddenly have anything to do with the young man in that house?"

After she had come home, and because she began to feel so ashamed of herself in the presence of other people, she had decided she would join a church, a decision that had pleased her father, who was a devout church member. The whole incident had in fact drawn her and her father closer together. Perhaps that was because, unlike her mother, he never bothered her with embarrassing questions.

Anyway she had made up her mind that if she ever married she would try to make her marriage a pure thing, based on comradeship, and she had felt that after all she must marry John Webster if he ever repeated his proposal of marriage. After what had happened that was the only right thing for them both to do and now that they were married it would be right also for them to try and make up for the past by leading clean pure lives and trying never to give way to the animal impulses that shocked and frightened people.

John Webster was standing facing his wife and daughter and his mind had gone back to the first night in bed with his wife and to the many other nights they had spent together. On that first night, long ago, when she lay talking to him, the moonlight came in through a window and fell on her face. She had been very beautiful at the moment. Now that he no longer approached her, afire with passion, but lay quietly beside her, with her body drawn a little away and with his arm about her shoulders, she was not afraid of him and occasionally put up her hand and touched his face. The truth was that he had got the notion into his head that there was in her a kind of spiritual power divorced altogether from the flesh. Outside the house, along the river banks, frogs were calling their throaty calls and once in the night some strange weird call came out of the air. That must have been some night bird, perhaps a loon. The sound wasn't a call, really. It was a kind of wild laugh. From another part of the house, on the same floor there came the sound of her uncle's snoring.

The two people had slept little. There was so much to say. After all they were hardly acquainted. What he thought at the time was that she wasn't a woman after all. She was a child. Something dreadful had happened to the child and he was to blame and now that she was his wife he would try hard to make everything all right. If passion frightened her he would subdue his passions. A thought had got into his head that had stayed there for years. It was that spiritual love was stronger and purer than physical love, that they were two different and distinct things. He had felt quite exalted when that notion came. He wondered now, as he stood looking down at the figure of his wife, what had happened that the notion at one time so strong in him, had not enabled him or her to get happiness together. One said the words and then, after all, they did not*mean anything. They were trick words of the sort that were always fooling people, forcing people into false positions. He had come to hate such words. "Now I accept the flesh first, all flesh," he thought vaguely, still looking down at her. He turned and stepped across the room to look in a glass. The flame of the candles made light enough so that he could see himself quite distinctly. It was a rather puzzling notion, but the truth was, that every time he had looked at his wife during the last few weeks he had wanted to run at once and look at himself in a glass.* He had wanted to assure himself of something. The tall slender girl who had once lain beside him in a bed, with the moonlight falling on her face, had become the heavy inert woman now in the room with him, the woman who was at this moment crouched on the floor in the doorway at the foot of the bed. How much had he become like that?

One didn't escape animalism so easily. Now the woman on the floor was so much more like an animal than himself. Perhaps the very sins he had committed, his shamefaced running off sometimes to other women in the cities, had saved him. "That would be a pronouncement to throw into the teeth of the good pure people if it were true," he thought with a quick inner throb of satisfaction.

The woman on the floor was like a heavy animal that had suddenly become very ill. He stepped back to the bed and looked at her with a queer impersonal light in his eyes. She had difficulty holding up her head. The light from the candles, cut off from her submerged body by the bed itself shone full on her face and shoulders. The rest of her body was buried in a kind of darkness. His mind remained the alert swift thing it had been ever since he had found Natalie. In a moment now he could do more thinking than he had done before in a year. If he ever became a writer, as he sometimes thought maybe he would, after he had gone away with Natalie, he would never want for things to write about. If one kept the lid off the well of thinking within oneself, let the well empty itself, let the mind consciously think any thoughts that came to it, accepted all thinking, all imaginings, as one accepted the flesh of people, animals, birds, trees, plants, one might live a hundred or a thousand lives in one life. To be sure it was absurd to go stretching things too much, but one could at least play with the notion that one could become something more than just one individual man and woman living one narrow circumscribed life. One could tear down all walls and fences and walk in and out of many people, become many people. One might in oneself become a whole town full of people, a city, a nation.

The thing to bear in mind however now, at this moment,*was the woman on the floor, the woman whose voice had, but a moment before called out again the word her lips had always been saying to him.

"Don't! Don't! Let's not, John! Not now, John!" What persistent denial, of himself, perhaps of herself, too, there had been.

It was rather absurdly cruel how impersonal he felt toward her. It was likely few people in the world ever realized what depths of cruelty lay sleeping within themselves. All the things that came out of the well of thinking within oneself, when one jerked off the lid, were not easy to accept as a part of oneself.

As for the woman on the floor, if one let one's* fancy go, one could stand as he was now doing, looking directly at the woman,* and could think the most absurdly inconsequential thoughts.

For one thing one could have the fancy that the darkness in which her body was submerged, because

191

of the accident that the light from the candles did not fall on it, was the sea of silence into which she had, all through these years, been sinking herself deeper and deeper.

And the sea of silence was just another and fancier name for something else, for that deep well within all men and women, of which he had been thinking so much during the last few weeks.

The woman who had been his wife, all people for that matter, spent their entire lives sinking themselves deeper and deeper into that sea. If one wanted to let oneself get more and more fancy about the matter, indulge in a kind of drunken debauch of fancy, as it were, one could in a half playful mood jump over some invisible line and say that the sea of silence into which people were always so intent on sinking themselves was in reality death. There was a race toward the goal of death between the mind and body and almost always the mind arrived first.

The race began in childhood and never stopped until either the body or mind had worn itself out and stopped working. Every one carried about, all the time, within himself life and death. There were two Gods sitting on two thrones. One could worship either, but in general mankind had preferred kneeling before death.

The god of denial had won the victory. To reach his throne-room one went through long hallways of evasion. That was the road to his throne-room, the road of evasion. One twisted and turned, felt one's*way in the darkness.   There were no sudden and blinding flashes of light.

John Webster had got a notion regarding his wife.   It was sure the heavy inert woman, now looking up into his face from the darkness of the floor, unable to speak to him, had little or nothing to do with a slender girl he had once married.   For one thing how utterly unlike they were physically.   It wasn't the same woman at all.   He could see that. Anyone who had looked at the two women could see that they had really nothing physically in common. But did she know that, had she ever thought of that, had she been, in any but a very superficial way, aware of the changes that had taken place in her? He decided she had not.   There was a kind of blindness common to almost all people.   The thing called beauty, men sought in woman, and that women, although they did not speak of it so often, were also looking for in men wasn't a thing that remained.   When it existed at all it came to people only in flashes.   One came into the presence of another and the flash came.   How confusing that was. Strange things like marriages followed.   "Until death do us part."   Well, that was all right too. One had to try to get things straight if one could. When one clutched at the thing called beauty in another, death always came, bobbing its head up too.*

How many marriages among peoples!   John Webster's mind was flying about.   He stood looking at the woman who, although they had separated long before—they had really and irrevocably separated one day on a hill above a valley in the state of Kentucky—was still in an odd way bound to him, and there was another woman who was his daughter in the same room.* The daughter stood beside him. He could put out his hand and touch her. She was not looking at himself or her mother, but at the floor. What was she thinking? What thoughts had he stirred up in her? What would be the result to her of the events of the night? There were things he couldn't answer, that he had to leave on the knees of the gods.

His mind was racing, racing. There were certain men he had always been seeing in the world. Usually they belonged to a class known as fellows with shaky reputations. What had happened to them? There were men who walked through life with a certain easy grace of manner. In some way they were beyond good and evil, stood outside the influences that made or unmade other men. John Webster had seen a few such men and had never been able to forget them. Now they passed, as in a procession, before his mind's eyes.

There was an old man with a white beard who carried a heavy walking stick and was followed by a dog. He had broad shoulders and walked with a certain stride. John Webster had encountered the man once, as he himself drove on a dusty country road. Who was the fellow? Where was he going? There was about him a certain air. "Go to the devil then," his manner seemed to say. "I'm a man walking here. Within me there is kingship. Go prattle of democracy and equality if you will,

194

worry your silly heads about a life after death, make up little lies to cheer your way in the darkness, but get out of my way. I walk in the light."

It might be all just a silly notion, what John Webster was now thinking about an old man he had once met walking on a country road. It was certain he remembered the figure with extraordinary sharpness. He had stopped his horse to gaze after the old man, who had not even bothered to turn and look at him. Well the old man had walked with a kingly stride. Perhaps that was the reason he had attracted John Webster's attention.

Now he was thinking of him and a few other such men he had seen during his life. There was one, a sailor who had come down to a wharf in the city of Philadelphia. John Webster was in that city on business and having nothing to do one afternoon had gone down to where the ships were loaded and unloaded.* A sailing vessel, a brigantine, lay at the wharf, and the man he had seen came down to it. He had a bag over his shoulder, containing perhaps his sea clothes. He was no doubt a sailor, about to sail before the mast on the brigantine. What he did was simply to come to the vessel's side, throw his bag aboard, call to another man who put his head out at a cabin door, and turning walked away.

But who had taught him to walk like that? The old Harry! Most men, and women too, crept through life like sneaks. What gave them the sense of being such underlings, such dogs? Were they constantly besmearing themselves with accusations of guilt and, if that was it, what made them do it?

The old man in the road, the sailor walking off along a street, a negro prize fighter he had once seen driving an automobile, a gambler at the horse races in a Southern city, who walked wearing a loud checkered vest before a grandstand filled with people, a woman actress he had once seen coming out at the stage entrance of a theatre, reprobates all perhaps and all walking with the stride of kings.

What had given such men and women this respect for themselves? It was apparent respect for self must be at the bottom of the matter. Perhaps they hadn't at all the sense of guilt and shame that had made of the slender girl he had once married the heavy inarticulate woman now squatted so grotesquely on the floor at his feet. One could imagine some such person as he had in mind saying to himself, "Well, here I am, you see, in the world. I have this long or short body, this brown or yellow hair. My eyes are of a certain color. I eat food, I sleep at night. I shall have to spend the whole of my life going about among people in this body of mine. Shall I crawl before them or shall I walk upright like a king? Shall I hate and fear my own body, this house in which I must live, or shall I respect and care for it? Well, the devil! The question is not worth answering. I shall take life as it offers itself. For me the birds shall sing, the green spread itself over the earth in the spring, for me the cherry tree in the orchard shall bloom."

John Webster had a fanciful picture of the man of his fancy going into a room. He closed the door. A row of candles stood on a mantle above a fireplace. The man opened a box and took from it a silver crown. Then he laughed softly and put the crown on his own head. "I crown myself a man," he said.

It was amazing. One was in a room looking at a woman who had been one's wife, and one was about to set out on a journey and would not see her again. Of a sudden there was a blinding rush of thoughts. One's fancy played far and wide. One seemed to have been standing in one spot thinking thoughts for hours, but in reality only a few seconds had passed since the voice of his wife, calling out that word, "don't," had interrupted his own voice telling a tale of an ordinary unsuccessful marriage.

The thing now was to keep his daughter in mind. He had better get her out of the room now. She was moving toward the door to her own room and in a moment would be gone. He turned away from the white-faced woman on the floor and watched his daughter. Now his own body was thrust between the bodies of the two women. They could not see each other.

There was a story of a marriage he had not finished, would never finish telling now, but in time his daughter would come to understand what the end of the story must inevitably be.

There was something that should be thought of now. His daughter was going out of his presence. Perhaps he would never see her again. One continually dramatized life, made a play of it. That was inevitable. Every day of one's life consisted of a series of little dramas and*one was always casting oneself for an important part in the performance. It was annoying to forget one's lines, not to walk out upon the stage when one had got one's cue. Nero fiddled when Rome was burning. He had forgotten what part he had assigned to himself and so fiddled in order not to give himself away. Perhaps he had intended making an ordinary politician's speech about a city rising again from the flames.

Blood of the saints! Would his daughter walk calmly out of the room without turning at the door? What had he yet intended saying to her? He was growing a little nervous and upset.

His daughter was standing in the doorway leading to her own room, looking at him, and there was a kind of intense half-insane mood in her as all evening there had been in him. He had infected her with something out of himself. After all there had been what he had wanted, a real marriage. After this evening the younger woman could never be what she might have been, had this evening not happened. Now he knew what he wanted for her. Those men, whose figures had just visited his fancy, the race-track man, the old man in the road, the sailor on the docks, there was a thing they had got hold of he had wanted her to have hold of too.

Now he was going away with Natalie, with his own woman, and he would not see his daughter again. She was a young girl yet, really. All of womanhood lay before her.

"I'm damned. I'm crazy as a loon," he thought. He had suddenly a ridiculous desire to begin singing a silly refrain that had just come into his head.

Diddle de di do,
Diddle de di do,
Chinaberries grow on a Chinaberry tree.
Diddle de di do.

And then his fingers, fumbling about in his pockets, came upon the thing he had unconsciously been looking for. He clutched it, half convulsively, and went toward his daughter, holding it between his thumb and finger.

On the afternoon of the day, on which he had first found his way in at the door of Natalie's house, and when he had become almost distracted from much thinking, he had found a bright little stone on the railroad track near his factory.

When one tried to think his way along a too difficult road one was likely, at any moment, to get lost. One went up some dark lonely road and then, becoming frightened, one became at the same time shrill and distracted. There were things to be done, but one could do nothing. For example, and at the most vital moment in life, one might spoil everything by beginning to sing a silly song. Others would throw up their hands. "He's crazy," they would say, as though such a saying ever meant anything at all.

Well, once before, he had been, as he was now,

at just this moment. Too much thinking had upset him. The door of Natalie's house had been opened and he had been afraid to enter. He had planned to run away from her, go to the city and get drunk and write her a letter telling her to go away to where he would not have to see her again. He had thought he preferred to walk in loneliness and darkness, to take the road of evasion to the throne-room of the god Death.

And at the moment all this was going on his eye had caught the glint of a little green stone lying among all the gray meaningless stones in the gravel bed of a railroad track. That was in the late afternoon and the sun's rays had been caught and reflected by the little stone.

He had picked it up and the simple act of doing so had broken a kind of absurd determination within him. His fancy, unable at the moment to play over the facts of his life, had played over the stone. A man's fancy, the creative thing within him, was in reality intended to be a healing thing, a supplementary and healing influence to the working of the mind. Men sometimes did a thing they called, "going it blind," and at such moments did the least blind acts of their whole lives. The truth was that the mind working alone was but a one-sided, maimed thing.

"Hito, tito,*there's no use my trying to become a philosopher." John Webster was stepping toward his daughter who was waiting for him to say or do something that had not yet been done. Now he was quite all right again. Some minute re-adjustment had taken place inside himself as it had on so many other occasions within the last few weeks.

Something like a gay mood had come over him. "In one evening I have managed to plunge pretty deeply down into the sea of life," he thought.

He became a little vain. There he was, a man of the middle class, who had lived all his life in a Wisconsin industrial town. But a few weeks before he had been but a colorless fellow in an almost altogether colorless world.* For years he had been going along, just so, day after day, week after week, year after year, going along streets, passing people in the streets, picking his feet up and setting them down, thump thump, eating food, sleeping, borrowing money at banks, dictating letters in offices, going along, thump thump, not daring to think or feel much of anything at all.

Now he could think more thoughts, have more fancies, while he took three or four steps across a room toward his daughter, than he had sometimes dared do in a whole year of his former life. There was a picture of himself in his fancy now that he liked.

In the fanciful picture he had climbed up to a high place above the sea and had taken off his clothes. Then he had run to the end of a cliff and had leaped off into space. His body, his own white body, the same body in which he had been living all through these dead years, was now making a long graceful arched curve against a blue sky.

That was rather nice too. It made a picture for the mind to take hold of and it was pleasant to think of one's body as making sharp striking pictures.

He had plunged far down into the sea of lives, into the clear warm still sea of Natalie's life, into the heavy salt dead sea of his wife's life, into the swiftly running young river of life that was in his daughter Jane.

"I'm a great little mixer-up of figures of speech, but at the same time I'm a great little swimmer in seas," he said aloud to his daughter.

Well, he had better be a little careful too. Her eyes were becoming puzzled again. It would take a long time for one, living with another, to become used to the sight of things jerked suddenly up out of the wells of thought within oneself and he and his daughter would perhaps never live together again.

He looked at the little stone held so firmly between his thumb and finger. It would be better to keep his mind fastened upon that now. It was a small, a minute thing, but one could fancy it looming large on the surface of a calm sea. His daughter's life was a river running down to the sea of life. She would want something to which she could cling when she had been cast out into the sea. What an absurd notion. A little green stone would not float in the sea. It would sink. He smiled knowingly.

There was the little stone held before him, in his extended hand. He had picked it up on a railroad track one day and had indulged in fancies concerning it and the fancies had healed him. By indulging in fancies concerning inanimate objects, one in a strange way glorified them. For example a man might go to live in a room. There was a picture in a frame on a wall, the walls of a room, an old desk, two candles under a Virgin, and a man's fancy made the place a sacred place. All the art of life perhaps consisted in just letting the fancy wash over and color*the facts of life.

The light from the two candles under the Virgin fell on the stone he held before him. It was about the size and shape of a small bean and was dark green in color.* In certain lights its color* changed swiftly. There was a flash of yellow green as of new grown things just coming out of the ground and then that faded away and the stone became altogether a dark lusty green, as of the leaves of oak trees in the late summer, one could fancy.

How clearly John Webster had remembered everything now. The stone he had found on the railroad track had been lost by a woman who was travelling west. The woman had worn it among other stones in a brooch at her throat. He remembered how his imagination had created her at the moment.

Or had it been set in a ring and worn on her finger?

Things were a bit mixed. Now he saw the woman quite clearly, as he had seen her in fancy once before, but she was not on a train, but was standing on a hill. It was winter and the hill was coated with a light blanket of snow and below the hill, in a valley, was a wide river covered with a shining sheet of ice. A man, a middle-aged, rather heavy-looking man stood beside the woman and she was pointing at something in the distance. The stone was set in a ring worn on the extended finger.

Now everything became very clear to John Webster. He knew now what he wanted. The woman on the hill was one of the strange people, like the sailor who had come down to the ship, the old man in the road, the actress coming out of the stage door of the theatre, one of the people who had crowned themselves with the crown of life.

He stepped to his daughter and, taking her hand, opened it and laid the little stone on her palm. Then he carefully closed her fingers until her hand was a fist.

He smiled, a knowing little smile and looked into her eyes. "Well, now Jane, it's pretty hard to tell you what I'm thinking," he said. "You see, there are a lot of things* in me I can't get out without time and now I'm going away. I want to give you something."

He hesitated. "This stone," he began again, "it's something for you to cling to perhaps, yes, that's it. In moments of doubt cling to it. When you become almost distracted and do not know what to do hold it in your hand."

He turned his head and his eyes seemed to be taking in the room slowly, carefully, as though not wanting to forget anything that made a part of the picture in which he and his daughter were now the central figures.

"As a matter of fact," he began again, "a woman, a beautiful woman might, you see, hold many jewels in her hand. She might have many loves, you see, and the jewels might be the jewels of experience, the challenges of life she had met, eh?"

John Webster seemed to be playing some fanciful game with his daughter, but now she was no longer frightened, as when she had first come into the room, or puzzled as she had been but a moment before. She was absorbed in what he was saying. The woman crouched on the floor behind her father was forgotten.

"There's one thing I shall have to do before I go away. I've got to give you a name for this little stone," he said, still smiling. Opening her hand again he took it out and went and stood for a moment holding it before one of the candles. Then he returned to her and again put it into her hand.

"It is from your father, but he is giving it to you at the moment when he is no longer being your father and has begun to love you as a woman. Well, I guess you'd better cling to it, Jane. You'll need it, God knows. If you want a name for it call it the 'Jewel of Life,' " he said and then, as though he had already forgotten the incident he put his hand on her arm and pushing her gently through the door closed it behind her.

IX

THERE still remained something for John Webster to do in the room. When his daughter had gone he picked up his bag and went out into the hallway as though about to leave without more words to the* wife, who still sat on the floor with her head hanging down, as though unaware of any life about her.

When he had got into the hallway and had closed the door he set his bag down and came back.* As he stood within the room, with the knob still held in his hand, he heard a noise on the floor below. "That's Katherine. What's she doing up at this time of the night?" he thought. He took out his watch and went nearer the burning candles. It was fifteen minutes to three. "We'll catch the early morning train at four all right," he thought.

There was his wife, or rather the woman who for so long a time had been his wife, on the floor at the foot of the bed. Now her eyes were looking directly at him. Still the eyes had nothing to say. They did not even plead with him. There was in them something that was hopelessly puzzled. If the events that had transpired in the room that night had torn the lid off the well she carried about within herself she had managed to clamp it back on again.

206

Now perhaps the lid would never again stir from its place.* John Webster felt peculiarly like he fancied an undertaker might feel on* being called at night into the presence of a dead body.

"The devil! Such fellows perhaps had no such feelings." Quite unconscious of what he was doing he took out a cigarette and lit it. He felt strangely impersonal; like one watching a rehearsal for some play in which one is not particularly interested. "It's a time of death all right," he thought. "The woman is dying. I can't say whether or not her body is dying but there's something within her that has already died." He wondered if he had killed her, but had no sense of guilt in the matter.

He went to stand at the foot of the bed and, putting his hand on the railing, leaned over to look at her.

It was a time of darkness. A shiver ran through his body and dark thoughts like flocks of blackbirds flew across the field of his fancy.

"The devil! There's a hell too! There's such a thing as death, as well as such a thing as life," he told himself. Here was however an amazing and quite interesting fact too. It had taken a long time and much grim determination for the woman on the floor before him to find her way along the road to the throne-room of death. "Perhaps no one, while there is life within him* to lift the lid, ever becomes quite submerged in the swamp of decaying flesh," he thought.

Thoughts stirred within John Webster that had not come to his mind in years. As a young man in college he must really have been more alive than he knew at the time. Things he had heard discussed by other young men, fellows who had a taste for literature, and that he had read in the books, the reading of which were a part of his duties, had all through the last few weeks been coming back to his mind. "One might almost think I had followed such things all my life," he thought.

The poet Dante, Milton, with his "Paradise Lost,"*the Hebrew poets of the older Testaments, all such fellows must at some time in their lives have seen what he was seeing at just this moment.

There was a woman on the floor before him and her eyes were looking directly into his. All evening there had been something struggling within her, something that wanted to come out to him and to her daughter.* Now the struggle was at an end. There was surrender. He kept looking down at her with a strange fixed stare in his own eyes.

"It's too late. It didn't work," he said slowly. He did not say the words aloud, but whispered them.

A new thought came. All through his life with this woman there had been a notion to which he had clung. It had been a kind of beacon that now he felt had from the first led him into a false trail. He had in some way picked up the notion from others about him. It was peculiarly an American notion, always being indirectly repeated in newspapers, magazines and books. Back of it was an insane, wishy-washy philosophy of life. "All things work together for good. God's in his Heaven, all's right with the world. All men are created free and equal."

"What an ungodly lot of noisy meaningless sayings*drummed into the ears of men and women trying to live their lives!"

A great disgust swept over him. "Well, there's no use my staying here any longer. My life in this house has come to an end," he thought.

He walked to the door and when he had opened it turned again. "Good night and good bye," he said as cheerfully as though he were just leaving the house in the morning for a day at the factory.

And then the sound of the door closing made a sharp jarring break in the silence of the house.*

BOOK FOUR

I

THE spirit of death was no doubt lurking in the Webster house. Jane Webster felt its presence. She had suddenly been made aware of the possibility of feeling, within herself, many unspoken, unannounced things. When her father had put his hand on her arm and had pushed her back into the darkness behind the closed door of her own room, she had gone directly to her bed and had thrown herself down on top of the bed covers. Now she lay clutching the little stone he had given her. How glad she was to have that something to clutch. Her fingers pressed against it so that it had already become imbedded in the flesh of her palm. If her life had been, until this evening, a quiet river, running down through fields toward the sea of life, it would be that no more. Now the river had come into a dark stony country. It ran now along rocky passageways, between high dark cliffs. What things might not now happen to her on the morrow, on the day after to-morrow. Her father was going away with a strange woman. There would be a scandal in the town. All her young women and men friends would look at her with a question in their eyes. Perhaps they would pity her. Her spirit rose up and the thought made her squirm with

213

anger. It was odd, but it was nevertheless true, that she had no particular feeling of sympathy for her mother. Her father had managed to bring himself close to her. In a queer way she understood what he was going to do, why he was doing it. She kept seeing the naked figure of the man striding up and down before her. There had always, since she could remember, been in her a kind of curiosity regarding men's bodies.

Once or twice, with young girls she knew well, there had been talk of the matter, guarded, half-frightened talk. "A man was so and so. It was quite dreadful what happened when one grew up and got married." One of the girls had seen something. There was a man lived near her, on the same street, and he wasn't always careful about pulling the shade to his bedroom window. One summer afternoon the girl was in her room, lying on her bed, and the man came into his room and took off all his clothes. He was up to some foolishness. There was a looking glass and he pranced up and down before it. He must have been pretending he was fighting the man he saw reflected in the glass as he kept advancing and receding and making the funniest movements with his body and arms. He lunged and scowled and struck out with his fists and then jumped back, as though the man in the glass had struck at him.

The girl on the bed had seen everything, all the man's body. At first she thought she would run out of the room and then she made up her mind to

214

stay. Well, she didn't want her mother to know what she had seen so she got up softly and crept along the floor to lock the door, so that her mother or a servant could not come suddenly in. What the girl had thought was that one had to find out things sometime and might as well take the chance that offered. It was dreadful and she had been unable to sleep for two or three nights after it happened but just the same she was glad she had looked. One couldn't always be a ninny and not know anything.

As Jane Webster lay on the bed with her fingers pressed down upon the stone her father had given her, the girl, talking of the naked man she had seen in the next house, seemed very young and unsophisticated. She felt a kind of contempt for her. As for herself, she had been in the actual presence of a naked man and the man had been seated beside her and had put his arm about her. His hands had actually touched the flesh of her own body. In the future, whatever happened, men would not be to her as they had been, and as they were to the young women who had been her friends. Now she would know about men as she hadn't before and would not be afraid of them. Of that she was glad. Her father's going away with a strange woman and the scandal that would no doubt spring up in the town might ruin the quiet security in which she had always lived but there had been much gained. Now the river that was her life was running through dark passageways. It would perhaps be plunged down over sharp jutting rocks.

It is, to be sure, false to credit Jane Webster with such definite thoughts although later, when she remembered that evening her own mind would begin to build a tower of romance about it. She lay on her bed clutching the little stone and was frightened but at the same time strangely glad.

Something had been torn open, perhaps the door out into life for her. There was a feeling of death in the Webster house but in her was a new sense of life and a glad new feeling of being unafraid of life.

Her father went down the stairway and into the dark hallway below, carrying his bag and thinking of death too.

Now there was no end to the elaboration of thinking that went on within John Webster. In the future he would be a weaver, weaving designs out of threads of thought. Death was a thing, like life, that came to people suddenly, that flashed in upon them. There were always the two figures walking through towns and cities, going in and out of houses, in and out of factories and stores, visiting lonely farmhouses at night, walking in the light of day along gay city streets, getting on and off trains, always on the move, appearing before people at the most unexpected moments. It might be somewhat difficult for a man to learn to go in and out of other people but for the two gods, Life and Death, there was no difficulty.

There was a deep well within every man and woman and when Life came in at the door of the house, that was the body, it reached down and tore the heavy iron lid off the well. Dark hidden things, festering in the well, came out and found expression for themselves, and the miracle was that, expressed, they became often very beautiful. There was a cleansing, a strange sort of renewal within the house of the man or woman when the god Life had come in.

As for Death and his entrance, that was another matter. Death had many strange tricks to play on people too. Sometimes he let their bodies live for a long time while he satisfied himself with merely clamping the lid down on the well within. It was as though he had said, "Well, there is no great hurry about physical death. That will come as an inevitable thing in its time. There is a much more ironic and subtle game to be played against my opponent Life. I will fill the cities with the damp fetid smell of death while the very dead think they are still alive. As for myself, I am the crafty one. I am like a great and subtile king, every one serves, while he talks only of freedom and leads his subjects to think it is he who serves, instead of themselves. I am like a great general, having always at his command, ready to spring to arms at the least sign from himself, a vast army of men."

John Webster went along the dark hallway below to the door leading into the street and had put his hand on the knob of the outer door when, instead of passing directly out, he stopped and reflected a moment. He was somewhat vain of the thoughts he had been having. "Perhaps I am a poet. Perhaps it's only the poet who manages to keep the lid off the well within and to keep alive up to the last minute before his body has become worn out and he must get out of it," he thought.

His vain mood passed and he turned and looked with a curious awareness along the hallway. At the moment he was much like an animal, moving in a dark wood, who, without hearing anything, is nevertheless aware there is life stirring, perhaps waiting for him, near at hand. Could that be the figure of a woman he saw, sitting within a few feet of him? There was a small old-fashioned hat-rack in the hallway near the front door and the lower part of it made a kind of seat on which one might sit.

One might fancy there was a woman sitting quietly there. She also had a bag packed and it was sitting on the floor beside her.

The old Harry! John Webster was a little startled. Was his fancy getting a little out of hand? There could be no doubt that there was a woman sitting there, within a few feet of where he stood, with the knob of the door in his hand.

He was tempted to put out his hand and see if he could touch the woman's face. He had been thinking of the two gods, Life and Death. No doubt an illusion had been created in his mind. There was this deep sense of a presence, sitting silently there, on the lower part of the hat-rack. He stepped a little nearer and a shiver ran through his body. There was a dark mass, making crudely the outlines of a human body, and as he stood looking it seemed to him that a face began to be more and more sharply outlined. The face, like the faces of two other women that had, at important and unexpected moments in his life, floated up before him, the face of a young naked girl on a bed in the long ago, the face of Natalie Swartz, seen in the darkness of a field at night, as he lay beside her—these faces had seemed to float up to him as though coming toward him out of the deep waters of a sea.

He had, no doubt, let himself become a little overwrought. One did not step lightly along the road he had been travelling. He had dared set out upon the road of lives and had tried to take others with him. No doubt he had been more worked up and excited than he had realized.

He put out his hand softly and touched the face that now appeared to come floating toward him out of darkness. Then he sprang back, striking his head against the opposite wall of the hallway. His fingers had encountered warm flesh. There was a terrific sensation of something whirling within his brain. Had he gone quite insane? A comforting thought came, flashing across the confusion of his mind.

"Katherine," he said in a loud voice. It was a kind of call out of himself.

"Yes," a woman's voice answered quietly, "I

wasn't going to let you go away without saying good bye."

The woman, who had for so many years been a servant in his house, explained her presence there in the darkness. "I'm sorry I startled you," she said. "I was just going to speak. You are going away and so am I. I've got everything packed and ready. I went up the stairs to-night and heard you say you were leaving so I came down and did my own packing. It didn't take me long. I didn't have many things to pack."

John Webster opened the front door and asked her to come outside with him and for a few minutes they stood talking together on the steps that led down from the front porch.

Outside the house he felt better. There was a kind of weakness, following the fright inside, and for a moment he sat on the steps while she stood waiting. Then the weakness passed and he arose. The night was clear and dark. He breathed deeply and there was a great relief in the thought that he would never again go through the door out of which he had just come. He felt very young and strong. Soon now, there would be a streak of light showing in the eastern sky. When he had got Natalie and they had climbed aboard a train they would sit in the day coach on the side that looked toward the East. It would be sweet to see the new day come. His fancy ran ahead of his body and he saw himself and the woman sitting together in the train. They would come into the lighted day coach from the darkness outside, just before dawn came. In the day coach people would have been asleep, folded up in the seats, looking uncomfortable and tired. The air would be heavy with the stale heaviness of breathing people confined in a close place. There would be the heavy acrid smell of clothes, that had for a long time absorbed the acids thrown off by bodies. He and Natalie would take the train as far as Chicago and get off there. Perhaps they would get on another train at once. It might be that they would stay in Chicago for a day or two. There would be plans to make, long hours of talk perhaps. There was a new life to begin now. He himself had to think what he wanted to do with his days. It was odd. He and Natalie had made no plans beyond getting on a train. Now for the first time his fancy tried to creep out beyond that moment, to penetrate into the future.

It was fine that the night had turned out clear. One would hate to set out, plodding off to the railroad station in the rain. How bright the stars were in the early morning hours. Now Katherine was talking. It would be well to listen to what she had to say.

She was telling him, with a kind of brutal frankness, that she did not like Mrs. Webster, had never liked her, and that she had only stayed in the house all these years as a servant because of himself.

He turned to look at her and her eyes were looking directly into his. They were standing very close together, almost as close as lovers might have stood, and, in the uncertain light, her eyes were strangely like Natalie's. In the darkness they appeared to glow as Natalie's eyes had seemed to glow on that night when he had lain with her in the field.

Was it only a chance that this new sense he had, of being able to refresh and rebuild himself by loving others, by going in and out at the open doors of the houses of others, had come to him through Natalie instead of through this woman Katherine? "Huh, it's marriage, every one is seeking marriage, that's what they are up to, seeking marriages," he told himself. There was something quiet and fine and strong in Katherine as in Natalie. Perhaps had he, at some moment, during all his dead unconscious years of living in the same house with her, but happened to have been alone with Katherine in a room, and had the doors to his own being opened at that moment, something might have transpired between himself and this woman that would have started within just such another revolution as the one through which he had been passing.

"That was possible too," he decided. "People would gain a lot if they could but learn to keep that thought in mind," he thought. His fancy played with the notion for a moment. One would walk through towns and cities, in and out of houses, into and out of the presence of people with a new feeling of respect if the notion should once get fixed in people's minds that, at any moment, anywhere, one was likely to come upon the one who carried before him as on a golden tray, the gift of life and the consciousness of life for his beloved.* Well, there was a picture to be borne in mind, a picture of a land and a people, cleanly arrayed, a people bearing gifts, a people who had learned the secret and the beauty of bestowing unasking love. Such a people would inevitably keep their own persons clean and well arrayed. They would be colorful people with a certain decorative sense, a certain awareness of themselves in relation to the houses in which they lived and the streets in which they walked. One could not love until one had cleansed and a little beautified one's own body and mind, until one had opened the doors of one's being and let in sun and air, until one had freed one's own mind and fancy. *

John Webster fought with himself now, striving to push his own thoughts and fancies into the background. There he was standing before the house in which he had lived all these years so near the woman Katherine and she was now talking to him of her own affairs. It was time now to give heed to her.

She was explaining how that, for a week or more, she had been aware of the fact that there was something wrong in the Webster household. One did not need to have been very sharp to have realized that. It was in the very air one breathed. The air of the house was heavy with it. As for herself, well she had thought John Webster had fallen in love with some woman other than Mrs. Webster. She had once been in love herself and the man she had loved had been killed. She knew about love.

On that night, hearing voices in the room above, she had crept up the stairs. She had not felt it was eavesdropping as she was directly concerned. Long ago when she was in trouble she had heard voices upstairs and she knew that in her hour of trouble John Webster had stood by her.

After that time, long ago, she had made up her mind that as long as he stayed in the house she would stay. One had to work and might as well work as a servant, but she had never felt close to Mrs. Webster. When one was a servant one sometimes had difficulty enough keeping up one's self-respect and the only way it could be done was by working for some one who also had self-respect. That was something few people seemed to understand. They thought people worked for money. As a matter of fact no one really worked for money. People only thought they did, maybe. To do so was to be a slave and she, Katherine, was no slave. She had money saved and besides she had a brother who owned a farm in Minnesota, who had several times written asking her to come and live with him. She intended to go there now but would not live in her brother's house. He was married and she did not intend to push herself into his household. As a matter of fact she would probably take the money she had saved and buy a small farm of her own.

"Anyway you're going away from this house to-night. I heard you say you were going with another woman and I thought I would go too," she said.

She became silent and stood looking at John Webster who was also looking at her, who was at the

224

moment absorbed in contemplation of her. In the uncertain light her face had become the face of a young girl. There was something about her face, at the moment, that suggested to his mind his daughter's face as she had looked at him in the dim light of the candles in the room upstairs. It was like that and at the same time it was like Natalie's face, as Natalie's face had been that afternoon in the office when he and she had first come close to each other, and as it had looked that other night in the darkness of the field.

One might so easily become confused. "It's all right about your going away, Katherine," he said aloud. "You know about that, what I mean is that you know what you want to do."

He stood in silence a moment, thinking. "It's like this, Katherine," he began again. "There's my daughter Jane upstairs. I'm going away but I can't take her with me any more than you can go live in your brother's house out there in Minnesota. I'm thinking that for the next two or three days or maybe for several weeks Jane is going to have a pretty hard time.

"There's no telling what will happen here." He made a gesture toward the house. "I'm going away but I suppose I've been counting on your being here until Jane gets on her own feet a little. You know what I mean, until she gets so she can stand alone."

On the bed upstairs Jane Webster's body was becoming more and more rigid and tense as she lay

225

listening to the undercurrent of noises in the house. There was a sound of movement in the next room. A door handle struck against a wall. The boards of the floor creaked. Her mother had been seated on the floor at the foot of the bed. Now she was getting up. She had put her hand on the railing of the bed to pull herself up. The bed moved a little. It moved on its rollers. There was a low rumbling sound. Would her mother come into her room? Jane Webster wanted no more words, no further explanations of what had happened to spoil the marriage between her mother and father. She wanted to be let alone now, to think her own thoughts. The thought that her mother might come into her bedroom frightened her. It was odd, she had now a sharp and distinct sense of the presence of death,* in some way connected with her mother's figure. To have the older woman come into her room now, even though no words were said, would be like having a ghost come. The thought of it happening made little creeping sensations run over the surface of her body. It was as though little soft hairy-legged creatures were running up and down her legs, up and down her back. She moved uneasily in the bed.

Her father had gone downstairs and along the hallway below but she had not heard the front door open and close. She lay listening for the sound of that, expecting it.

The house was silent, too silent. Somewhere, a long way off, there was the loud ticking of a clock. During the year before, when she had graduated from the town high school, her father had given her a small watch. It lay now on a dressing table at the further side of the room. Its rapid ticking was like some small creature, clad in steel shoes and running rapidly and with the shoes clicking together. The little creature was running swiftly along an endless hallway, running with a kind of mad sharp determination but never getting either nearer or further away. Into her mind there came a picture of a small imp-like boy with a wide grinning mouth and with pointed ears that stood straight up from his head like the ears of a fox terrier. Perhaps the notion had got into her head from some picture of Puck remembered from a childhood story book. She was conscious that the sound she heard came from the watch on the dresser but the picture in her mind stayed. The imp-like figure stood with his head and body motionless while his legs worked furiously. He grinned at her and his little steel-clad feet clicked together.

She tried consciously to relax her body. There were hours to be spent, lying thus on the bed, before another day came and she would have to face the problems of the new day. There would be things to face. Her father would have gone off with a strange woman. When she walked in the streets people would be looking at her. "That's his daughter," they would be saying. Perhaps, as long as she stayed in town, she could never again walk along streets unaware that she was being looked at, but on the other hand, perhaps she would not stay. There was a kind of exhilaration to be got from thinking of going off to strange places, perhaps to some large city, where she would always be walking about among strangers.

She was getting herself into a state and would have to take herself in hand. There were times, although she was young she had already known such times, when the mind and body seemed to have nothing at all to do with each other. One did things with the body, put it into bed, made it get up and walk about, made the eyes attempt to read pages in some book, did many kinds of things with the body, while the mind went on about its own affairs unheeding. It thought of things, fancied all manner of absurd things, went its own way.

At such times in the past Jane's mind had a trick of getting her body into the most absurd and startling situations, while it ran wild and free—did as it pleased. She was in bed in her room with the door closed but her fancy took her body out into the street. She went along conscious that all the men she passed were smiling and she kept wondering what was the matter. She hurried home and went to her room only to find that her dress was all unbuttoned at the back. It was terrible. Again she was walking in the street and the white drawers she wore under her skirts had become in some unaccountable way unfastened. There was a young man coming toward her. He was a new young man who had just come to town and had taken a job in a store. Well, he was going to speak to her. He raised his hat and at just that moment the drawers began to creep down along her legs.

Jane Webster lay in her bed and smiled at the memory of the fears that had visited her when, in the past, her mind had got into the trick of running wildly, uncontrolled. In the future things would be somewhat different. She had gone through something and had perhaps much more to go through. The things that had seemed so terrible would perhaps only be amusing now. She felt infinitely older, more sophisticated, than she had been but a few hours earlier.

How strange it was that the house remained so silent. From somewhere, off in the town, there came the sound of horses*hoofs on a hard road and the rattle of a wagon. A voice shouted, faintly. Some man of the town, a teamster, was setting out early. Perhaps he was going to another town to get a load of goods and haul them back. He must have a long way to go that he started out so early. She moved her shoulders uneasily. What was the matter with her? Was she afraid in her own bedroom, in her own bed? Of what was she afraid?

She sat suddenly and rigidly upright in bed and then, after a moment, let her body fall backward again. There had come a sharp cry out of the throat of her father, a cry that had gone ringing through the house. "Katherine," her father's voice cried. There was just that one word. It was the name of the Webster's one servant. What did her father want of Katherine? What had happened? Had something terrible happened in the house? Had something happened to her mother?

There was something lurking at the back of Jane Webster's mind, a thought that did not want to be expressed. It was as yet unable to make its way up out of the hidden parts of herself and into her mind.

The thing she feared, expected, could not have happened yet. Her mother was in the next room. She had just heard her moving about in there.

There was a new sound in the house. Her mother was moving heavily along the hallway just outside the bedroom door. The Websters had turned a small bedroom, at the end of the hall, into a bathroom and her mother was going in there. Her feet fell slowly, flatly, heavily and slowly, on the floor of the hallway. After all her feet only made that strange sound because she had put on her soft bedroom slippers.

Downstairs now, if one listened, one could hear voices saying words softly. That must be her father talking to the servant Katherine. What could he want of her? The front door opened and then closed again. She was afraid. Her body shook with fear. It was terrible of her father to go away and leave her alone in the house. Could he have taken the servant Katherine with him? The thought was unbearable. Why was she so afraid of the thought of being left alone in the house with her mother?

There was a thought lurking within her, deep within her, that did not want to get itself expressed. Something was about to happen to her mother, now, within a few minutes. One did not want to think about it. In the bathroom there were certain bottles, sitting on shelves in a little box-like cabinet. They were labeled poison. One hardly knew why they were kept there but Jane had seen them many times. She kept her toothbrush in a glass tumbler in the cabinet. One supposed the bottles contained medicines of the sort that was only to be taken externally. One did not think much of such matters, was not in the habit of thinking of them.

Now Jane was sitting upright in bed again. She was alone in the house with her mother. Even the servant Katherine had gone away. The house felt altogether cold and lonely, deserted. In the future she would always feel out of place in this house in which she had always lived and she would feel also, in some odd way, separated from her mother. To be alone with her mother would now, perhaps, always make her feel a little lonely.

Could it be that the servant Katherine was the woman with whom her father had planned to go away? That could not be. Katherine was a large heavy woman with big breasts and dark hair that was turning gray. One could not think of her as going away with a man. One thought of her as moving silently about a house and doing housework. Her father would be going away with a younger woman, with a woman not much older than herself.

One should get hold of oneself. When one got excited, let oneself go, the fancy sometimes played one strange and terrible tricks.

Her mother was in the bathroom, standing by the little box-like cabinet. Her face was pale, of a pasty paleness. She had to keep one hand against the wall to keep from falling. Her eyes were gray and heavy. There was no life in them. A heavy cloud-like film had passed over her eyes. It was like a heavy gray cloud over the blue of the sky. Her body rocked back and forth too. At any moment it might fall. But a short time ago, and even amid the strangeness of the adventure in her father's bedroom, things had seemed suddenly quite clear. She had understood things she had never understood before. Now nothing could be understood. There was a whirlpool of confused thoughts and actions into which one had been plunged.

Now her own body had begun to rock back and forth on the bed. The fingers of her right hand were clutched over the tiny stone her father had given her but she was, at the moment, unaware of the small round hard thing lying in her palm. Her fists kept beating her own body, her own legs and knees. There was something she wanted to do, something it was now right and proper she should do. It was the time now for her to scream, to jump off the bed, to run along the hallway to the bathroom and tear the bathroom door open. Her mother was about to do something one did not passively stand by and see done. She should be crying out at the top of her voice, crying for help. There was a word that should be on her lips now. "Don't, don't, don't," she should now be screaming.

Her lips should now be making the word ring through the house. She should be making the house and the street on which the house stood echo and reëcho with the word.

And she could say nothing. Her lips were sealed. Her body could not move from the bed. It could only rock back and forth on the bed.*

Her fancy kept on painting pictures, swift, vivid, terrible pictures.

There was, in the bathroom, in the cabinet, a bottle containing a brown liquid and her mother had put up her hand and had got hold of it. Now she had put it to her lips. She had swallowed all the contents of the bottle.

The liquid in the bottle was brown, of a reddish brownness. Before she had swallowed it her mother had lighted a gas light. It was directly above her head, as she stood facing the cabinet, and the light from it fell down over her face. There were little puffy red bags of flesh under the eyes and they looked strange and almost revolting against the pasty whiteness of the skin. The mouth was open and the lips were gray too. There was a reddish brown stain running down from one corner of the mouth, down over the chin. Some drops of the liquid had fallen on her mother's white nightgown. Convulsive spasms, as of pain, passed over the pasty white face. The eyes remained closed. There was a trembling quivering movement of the shoulders.

Jane's body continued to rock back and forth. The flesh of her body quivered too. Her body was

233

rigid. Her fists were closed, tight, tight. Her fists continued to beat down upon her legs. Her mother had managed to get out through the bathroom door and across the little hallway to her own room. She had thrown herself face-downward on her bed in the darkness. Had she thrown herself down or had she fallen? Was she dying now, would she die presently or was she already dead? In the next room, in the room where Jane had seen her father walking naked before her mother and herself, the candles were still burning, under the picture of the Virgin. There was no doubt the older woman would die. In fancy Jane had seen the label on the bottle that contained the brown liquid. It was marked "Poison." There was the picture of the skull and cross-bones druggists put on such bottles.

And now Jane's body had quit rocking. Perhaps her mother was dead. Now one tried to begin to think of other things. She became vaguely, but at the same time almost deliciously, conscious of some new element come into the air of the bedroom.

There was a pain in the palm of her right hand. Something hurt her and the sense of hurting was refreshing. It brought life back. There was consciousness of self in the realization of bodily pain. One's mind could start back along the road from some dark far place to which it had run crazily off. One's mind could take hold of the thought of the little hurt place in the soft flesh of the palm of the hand. There was something there, something hard and sharp that cut into the flesh of the palm when one's finger pressed down rigid and tense upon it.

II

In the palm of Jane Webster's hand lay the small green stone her father had picked up on the railroad tracks and had given her at the moment of his departure. "The Jewel of Life," he had called it in the moment when confusion had led him to give way to a desire to make some kind of gesture. A romantic notion had popped into his head. Had not men always used symbols to help carry them over the rough places in life? There was the Virgin with her candles. Was she not also a symbol? At some time, having decided in a moment of vanity that thought was of more importance than fancy, men had discarded the symbol. A Protestant kind of man arose who believed in a thing called "the age of reason." There was a dreadful kind of egotism. Men could trust their own minds. As though they knew anything at all of the workings of their own minds.

With a gesture and a smile John Webster had put the stone into his daughter's hand and now she was clinging to it. One could press the finger down hard upon it and feel in the soft palm of the hand this delicious and healing pain.

Jane Webster was trying to reconstruct something. In darkness she was trying to feel her way along the face of a wall. The wall had little sharp points sticking out that hurt the palm of the hand. If one followed the wall far enough one came to a lighted place. Perhaps the wall was studded with jewels, put there by others, who had groped their way along in the darkness.

Her father had gone away with a woman, with a young woman, much like herself. He would live with the woman now. Perhaps she would never see him again. Her mother was dead. In the future she would be alone in life. She would have to begin now and make a life of her own.

Was her mother dead or had she just been having terrible fancies?

One was plunged suddenly down from a high safe place into the sea and then one had to try to swim, to save oneself. Jane's mind began playing with the thought of herself as swimming in a sea.

During the summer of the year before she had gone with some young men and women on an excursion to a town facing Lake Michigan, and to a resort near the town.* There was a man who dived down into the sea from a tall tower, that had been stuck far up into the sky. He had been employed to dive in order to entertain the crowd but things had not turned out as they should. The day, for such an affair, should have been bright and clear, but in the morning it began to rain and in the afternoon it turned cold and the sky, covered with low heavy clouds, was heavy and cold too.

Cold gray clouds hurried across the sky. The

diver fell down from his high place into the sea, in the presence of a small silent crowd, but the sea did not receive him warmly. It awaited him in a cold gray silence. Looking at him, falling thus, sent a cold shiver through the body.

What was the cold gray sea toward which the man's naked body fell so swiftly?

On that day,* when the professional diver had taken his leap, Jane Webster's heart had stopped beating until he had gone down into the sea and his head had reappeared on the surface. She was standing beside a young man, her escort for the day, and her hands clutched eagerly his arm and shoulder. When the diver's head reappeared she put her head down on the young man's shoulder and her own shoulders shook with sobs.

It had, no doubt, been a very silly performance and she had been ashamed of it later. The diver was a professional. "He knows what he is about," the young man had said. Every one present had laughed at Jane and she had become angry because her escort had laughed too. Had he but had sense enough to know how she was feeling at the moment, she thought she would not have minded the others laughing.

"I'm a great little swimmer in seas."

It was altogether amazing how ideas, expressed in words, kept running from mind to mind. "I'm a great little swimmer in seas." But a short time before her father had said the words as she stood in the doorway between the two bedrooms and he came walking toward her. He had wanted to give her the stone, she now held pressed against the palm of her hand, and had wanted to say something about it, and instead of words regarding the stone, there had come to his lips these words about swimming in seas. There had been something puzzled and confused in his whole bearing at the moment. He had been upset, as she was now. The moment was now being lived over again, swiftly, in the daughter's mind. Her father was again stepping toward her, holding the stone between his thumb and finger, and the wavering, uncertain light had again come into his eyes. Quite distinctly, as though he were again in her presence, Jane heard again the words that, but such a short time before, had seemed without meaning, meaningless words come from the lips of a man temporarily drunk or insane, "I'm a great little swimmer in seas."

She had been plunged down from a high safe place, down into a sea of doubt and fear. Only a short time before, but yesterday, she had been standing on firm ground. One could let one's fancy play with the thought of what had happened to her. There would be a kind of comfort in doing that.

She had been standing on firm ground, high above a vast sea of confusion, and then, quite suddenly, she had been pushed off the firm high ground and down into the sea.

Now, at this very moment, she was falling down into the sea. Now a new life had to begin for her.

Her father had gone away with a strange woman and her mother was dead.

She was falling down off the high safe ground into the sea. With a kind of absurd flourish, as by a gesture of the arm, her own father had plunged her down. She was clad in her white nightgown and her falling figure made a white streak against the gray of cold skies.

Her father had put a meaningless little stone in her hand and had gone away and then her mother had gone into the bathroom and had done a terrible, an unthinkable thing, to herself.

And now she, Jane Webster, had gone quite down into the sea, far far down into a lonely cold gray place. She had gone down into the place from which all life came and to which, in the end, all life goes.

There was a heaviness, a deadly heaviness. All life had become gray and cold and old. One walked in darkness. One's body fell with a soft thump against gray soft unyielding walls.*

The house in which one lived was empty. It was an empty house in an empty street of an empty town. All the people Jane Webster had known, the young men and women with whom she had lived, with whom she had walked about on summer evenings, could not be a part of what she was facing now. Now she was quite alone. Her father had gone away and her mother had killed herself. There was no one. One walked alone in darkness. One's body struck with a soft thump against soft gray unyielding walls.

The little stone held so firmly in the palm of the hand hurt and hurt.

Before her father had given it to her he had gone to hold it up before the candle flame. In certain lights its color changed. Yellowish green lights came and went in it. The yellowish green lights were of the color of young growing things pushing their way up out of the damp and cold of frozen grounds, in the spring.

III

JANE WEBSTER was lying on the bed in the darkness of her room and crying. Her shoulders shook with sobs but she made no sound. Her finger, that had been pressed down so hard against her palms, had relaxed, but there was a spot, in the palm of her right hand, that burned with a warm feverishness. Her mind had become passive now. Fancy had released her from its grip. She was like a fretful and hungry child that has been fed and that lies quietly with its face turned to a white wall.

Her sobbing now indicated nothing. It was a release. She was a little ashamed of her lack of control over herself and kept putting up the hand, that held the stone, first closing it carefully that the precious stone be not lost, and with her fist wiping the tears away. What she wished, at the moment, was that she could become suddenly a strong resolute woman, able to handle quietly and firmly the situation that had arisen in the Webster household.

IV

THE servant Katherine was coming up the stairs. After all she was not the woman with whom Jane's father was going away. How heavy and resolute Katherine's footsteps were! One could be resolute and strong when one knew nothing of what had been going on in the house. One could walk thus, as though one*were going up the stairs of an ordinary house, in an ordinary street.

When Katherine put her foot down on one of the steps the house seemed to shake a little. Well, one could not say the house shook. That would be stretching things too much. What one was trying to express was just that Katherine was not very sensitive. She was one who made a direct frontal attack upon life. Had she been very sensitive she might have known something of the terrible things going on in the house without having to wait to be told.

Now Jane's mind was playing tricks on her again. An absurd sentence came into her mind.

"Wait until you see the whites of their eyes and then shoot."

It was silly, altogether silly and absurd, what notions were now racing through her head. Her father had set going in her the sometimes relentless and often unexplainable thing, represented by the released fancy. It was a thing that could color and beautify the facts of life but it could also, upon occasions, run on and on regardless of the facts of life. Jane believed she was in the house with the dead body of her mother, who had just committed suicide, and there was something within her that told her she should now give herself over to sadness. She did weep but her weeping had nothing to do with her mother's death. It did not take that into consideration. She was not, after all, so much sad as excited.

The weeping that had been silent was now audible all over the house. She was making a noise like a foolish child and was ashamed of herself. What would Katherine think of her?

"Wait until you see the whites of their eyes and then shoot."

What an utterly silly jumble of words. Where had they come from? Why were such mean-ingless silly words dancing in her brain at such a vital moment of her life? She had got them out of some book at school, a history book perhaps. Some general had shouted the words at his men as they stood waiting for an advancing enemy. And what had that to do with the fact of Katherine's footsteps on the stairs? In a moment Katherine would be coming into the room where she was.

She thought she knew exactly what she would do. She would get quietly out of bed and go to the door and admit the servant. Then she would strike a light.

She had, in fancy, a picture of herself, standing by a dressing table at the side of the room and addressing the servant calmly and resolutely. One had to begin a new life now. Yesterday perhaps one was a young woman with no experience in life but now one was a mature woman who had difficult problems to face. One had, not only the servant Katherine, but the whole town to face. Tomorrow one would be very much in the position of a general in command of troops that had to withstand an attack. One had to comport oneself with diginity.* There would be people who wanted to scold at her father, others who wanted to pity herself. Perhaps she would have to handle affairs too. There would be arrangements necessary, in connection with selling her father's factory and getting moneys so that she could go on and make plans for living her life. One could not be a silly child sitting and sobbing on a bed at such a moment.

And at the same time one could not, at such a tragic moment in life, and when the servant came in, suddenly burst out laughing. Why was it that the sound of Katherine's resolute footsteps on the stairs made her want to laugh and weep at the same time? "Soldiers advancing resolutely across an open field toward an enemy. Wait until you see the whites of their eyes." Silly notions. Silly words dancing in the brain. One did not want either to laugh or weep. One wanted to comport oneself with dignity.

An intensive struggle was going on within Jane Webster and now it had lost dignity and had become no more than a struggle to stop crying loudly, not to begin laughing, and to be ready to receive the servant Katherine with a certain dignity.

As the footsteps drew nearer the struggle intensified. Now she was again sitting very stiffly upright in the bed and again her body was rocking back and forth. Her fists, doubled and hard, were again beating down upon her legs.

Like every one else in the world Jane had been spending her entire life making dramatizations of herself in relation to life. One did that as a child and later as a young girl in school. One's mother died suddenly or one found oneself violently ill and facing death. Every one gathered about one's death-bed and all were amazed at the quiet dignity with which one met the situation.

Or again there was a young man who had smiled at one on the street. Perhaps he had the audacity to think of one as merely a child. Very well. Let the two of them be thrown together into a difficult position and then see which one could comport himself with the greater dignity.

There was something terrible about this whole situation. After all Jane felt she had it in her to carry life off with a kind of flourish. It was certain no other young woman of her acquaintance had ever been put into such a position as she was now in. Already, although they, as yet, knew nothing of what had occurred, the eyes of the whole town were directed toward herself and she was merely sitting in the darkness on a bed and sobbing like a child.

She began to laugh, sharply, hysterically, and then the laughter stopped and the loud sobbing began again. The servant Katherine came to her bed-room door but she did not knock and give Jane the chance to arise and receive her with dignity, but came right in. She ran across the room and knelt at the side of Jane's bed. Her impulsive action brought an end to Jane's desire to be the grand lady, at least for the night. The woman Katherine had become, by her quick impulsiveness, sister to something that was her own real self too. There were two women, shaken and in trouble, both deeply stirred by some inward storm, and clutching at each other in the darkness. For a time they stayed thus, on the bed, their arms about each other.

And so Katherine was not after all such a strong resolute person. One need not be afraid of her. That was an infinitely comforting thought to Jane. She also was weeping. Perhaps now, if Katherine were to jump up and begin walking about, one would not have the fancy about her strong resolute steps making the house shake. Had she been in Jane Webster's shoes perhaps she also would have been unable to get up out of bed and speak of everything that had happened calmly and with cool dignity. Why, Katherine also might have found herself unable to control the desire to weep and laugh loudly at the same time. Well, she was not such a terrible, such a strong resolute and terrible person, after all.

To the younger woman, sitting now in the dark-ness with her body pressed against the more sturdy body of the older woman there came a sweet intangible sense of being fed and refreshed out of the body of this other woman. She even gave way to a desire to put up her hand and touch Katherine's cheek. The older woman had great breasts against which one could cushion oneself. What comfort there was in her presence in the silent house.

Jane stopped weeping and felt suddenly weary and a little cold. "Let's not stay here. Let's go downstairs into my room," Katherine said. Could it be that she knew what had happened in that other bedroom? It was evident she did know. Then it was true. Jane's heart stopped beating and her body shook with fear. She stood in the darkness beside the bed and put her hand against the wall to keep from falling. She had been telling herself that her mother had taken poison and had killed herself but it was evident there was an inner part of her had not believed, had not dared believe.

Katherine had found a coat and was putting it about Jane's shoulders. It was odd, this being so cold when the night was comparatively warm.

The two women went out of the room into the hallway. A gas light was burning in the bathroom at the end of the hallway and the bathroom door had been left open.

Jane closed her eyes and clung to Katherine. The notion that her mother had killed herself had now become a certainty. It was so evident now that Katherine knew about it too. Before Jane's eyes the drama of the suicide again played itself out in the theatre of her fancy. Her mother was standing and facing the little cabinet fastened to the wall of the bathroom. Her face was turned upward and the light from above shone down on it. One hand was against the wall of the room to keep the body from falling and the other hand held a bottle. The face turned up to the light was white, of a pasty whiteness. It was a face that from long association had become familiar to Jane but it was at the same time strangely unfamiliar. The eyes were closed and there were little reddish bags of flesh under the eyes. The lips hung loosely open and from one corner of the mouth a reddish brown streak ran down over the chin. Some spots of a brown liquid had fallen down over the white nightgown.

Jane's body was trembling violently. "How cold the house has become, Katherine," she said and opened her eyes. They had reached the head of the stairs and from where they stood could look directly into the bathroom. There was a gray bath mat on the floor and a small brown bottle had been dropped on it. In passing out of the room the heavy foot of the woman, who had swallowed the contents of the bottle, had stepped on the bottle and had broken it. Perhaps her foot had been cut but she had not minded. "If there was pain, a hurt place, that would have been a comfort to her," Jane thought. In her hand she still held the stone her father had given her. How absurd that he should have called it "the Jewel of Life." There was a spot of yellowish green light reflected from an edge of the broken bottle on the floor of the bathroom. When her father had taken the little stone to the candle in the bedroom, and had held it up to the candle-light such another yellowish green light had flashed from it too. "If mother were still alive she would surely make some sound of life now. She would wonder what Katherine and I were doing tramping about the house and would get up and come to her bedroom door to inquire about it," she thought drearily.

When Katherine had put Jane into her own bed, in a little room off the kitchen, she went upstairs to make certain arrangements. There had been no explanations. In the kitchen she had left a light burning and the servant's bedroom was lighted by a reflected light, shining through an open doorway.

Katherine went to Mary Webster's bedroom and without knocking opened the door and went in. There had been a gas lamp lighted and the woman, who did not want any more of life, had tried to get into bed and die respectably between the sheets but had not been successful. The tall slender girl, who had once refused love on a hillside, had been taken by death before she had time to protest. Her body, half lying on the bed, had struggled and twisted itself about and had slipped off the bed to the floor. Katherine lifted it up and put it on the bed and went to get a wet cloth to cleanse the disfigured and discolored face.

Then a thought came to her and she put the cloth away. For a moment she stood in the room looking about. Her own face had become very white and she felt ill. She put out the light and going into John Webster's bedroom closed the door.

The candles were still burning beside the Virgin and she took the little framed picture and put it away, high up on a closet shelf. Then she blew out one of the candles and carried it, with the lighted one, downstairs and into the room where Jane lay waiting.

The servant went to a closet and getting an extra blanket wrapped it about Jane's shoulders. "I don't believe I'll undress," she said. "I'll come sit on the bed with you as I am."

"You have already figured it out," she said, in a matter of fact tone, when she had seated herself and when she had put her arm about Jane's shoulder. Both women were pale but Jane's body no longer trembled.

"If mother has died at least I have not been left alone in the house with the dead body," she thought gratefully. Katherine did not tell her any of the details of what she had found on the floor above. "She's dead," she said, and after the two had waited in silence for a moment she began to elaborate an idea that had come into her mind as she stood in the presence of the dead woman, in the bedroom above. "I don't suppose they'll try to connect your father with this but they may," she said thoughtfully. "I saw something like that happen once. A man died and after he was dead some men tried to make him out a thief. What I think is this— we had better sit here together until morning comes. Then I'll call in a doctor. We'll say we knew nothing of what had happened until I went to call your mother for breakfast. By that time, you see, your father will be gone."

The two women sat in silence close together, looking at the white wall of the bedroom. "I suppose we had both better remember that we heard mother moving about the house after father went away," Jane whispered presently. It was pleasant to be able to make herself, thus, a part of Katherine's plans to protect her father. Her eyes were shining now, and there was something of feverishness in her eagerness to understand everything clearly but she kept pressing her body close against the body of Katherine. In the palm of her hand she still held the stone her father had given her and now when her finger pressed down upon it even lightly there was a comforting throb of pain from the tender hurt place in her palm.

V

AND as the two women sat on the bed, John Webster walked through the silent deserted streets toward the railroad station with his new woman, Natalie.

"Well, the devil," he thought as he plodded along, "this has been a night! If the rest of my life is as busy as these last ten hours have been I'll be kept on the jump."

Natalie was walking in silence and carrying a bag. The houses along the street were all dark. There was a strip of grass between the brick sidewalk and the roadway and John Webster stepped over and walked upon it. He liked the idea of his feet making no sound as he escaped out of the town. How pleasant it would be if he and Natalie were winged things and could fly away unobserved in the darkness.

Now Natalie was weeping. Well that was all right. She did not weep audibly. John Webster did not, as a matter of fact, know for sure that she was weeping. Still he did know. "At any rate," he thought, "when she weeps she does the job with a certain dignity." He was himself in a rather impersonal mood. "There's no use thinking too much about what I've done. What's done is done.

I've begun a new life. I couldn't turn back now if I chose."

The houses along the street were dark and silent. The whole town was dark and silent. In the houses people were sleeping, dreaming all manner of absurd dreams, too.

Well he had expected he would run into some kind of a row at Natalie's house but nothing of the sort had happened. The old mother had been quite wonderful. John Webster half regretted he had never known her personally. There was something about the terrible old woman that was like himself. He smiled as he walked along on the strip of grass. "It may well be that in the end I will turn out an old reprobate, a regular old heller," he thought almost gaily.* His mind played with the idea. He had surely made a good start. Here he was, a man well past the middle age, and it was past midnight, almost morning, and he was walking in deserted streets with a woman with whom he was going away to live what was called an illegitimate life. "I started late but I'm proving a merry little upsetter of things now that I've started," he told himself.

It was really too bad that Natalie did not step off the brick sidewalk and walk on the grass. After all it was better, when one was setting out on new adventures, that one go swiftly and stealthily. There must be innumerable growling lions of respectability sleeping in the houses along the streets. "They're pure sweet people, such as I was when I used to go home from the washing machine

factory and sleep beside my wife*in the days when
we were newly married and had come back here to
live in this town," he thought sardonically. He
imagined innumerable people, men and women,
creeping into beds at night and sometimes talking
as he and his wife had so often talked. They had
always been covering something up, busily talking,
covering something up. "We made a big smoke of
talk about purity and sweetness of living, didn't we
though, eh?" he whispered to himself.

Well the people in the houses were asleep and he
did not wish to awaken them. It was too bad
Natalie was weeping. One couldn't disturb her in
her grief. That wouldn't be fair. He wished he
might speak to her and ask her to get off the sidewalk and walk silently on the grass along the roadway or at the edge of the lawns.

His mind turned back to the few moments at
Natalie's house. The devil! He had expected a
row there and nothing of the sort had happened.
When he got to the house, Natalie was waiting for
him. She was sitting by a window in a dark room,
downstairs in the Swartz cottage, and her bag was
packed and sitting beside her. She came to the
front door and opened it before he had time to
knock.

And there she was all ready to set out. She came
out carrying her bag and didn't say anything. As
a matter of fact she had not said anything to him
yet. She had just come out of the house and had
walked beside him to where they had to pass through

a gate to reach the street and then her mother and sister had come out and had stood on a little porch to watch them go.

How bully the old mother had been. She had even laughed at them. "Well, you two have got the gall. You tramp off as cool as two cucumbers, now don't you?" she had shouted. Then she had laughed again. "Do you know there's going to be a hell of a row about this all over town in the morning?" she asked. Natalie* hadn't answered her. "Well, good luck to you, you husky whore, trotting off with your damned reprobate," her mother had shouted, still laughing.

The two people had turned a corner and had passed out of sight of the Swartz house. No doubt there must be other people awake in other houses along the little street, and no doubt they had been listening and wondering. On two or three occasions some of the neighbors had wanted to have Natalie's mother arrested because of her foul language but they had been dissuaded by others, out of consideration for the daughters.

Was Natalie weeping now because she was leaving the old mother or was it because of the school-teacher* sister whom John Webster had never known?

He felt very like laughing at himself. As a matter of fact he knew little of Natalie or what she might be thinking or feeling at such a time. Had he only taken up with her because she was a kind of instrument that would help him escape from his wife and from a life he had come to detest? Was he but using her? Had he at bottom any real feeling in regard to her, any understanding of her?

He wondered.

One made a mighty big fuss, fixed up a room with candles and a picture of the Virgin, paraded oneself naked before women, got oneself little glass candle sticks with bronze-colored Christs on the Cross on them.

One made a great fuss, pretended one was upsetting the whole world, in order to do something that a man of real courage would have gone at in a direct simple way. Another man might have done everything he had done with a laugh and a gesture.

What was all this business he was up to anyway?

He was going away, he was deliberately walking out of his native town, walking out of a town in which he had been a respectable citizen for years, all his life in fact. He was going out of the town with a woman, younger than himself, who had taken his fancy.

The whole thing was a matter that could be easily enough understood, by anyone, by any man one might happen to meet in the street. At any rate every one would be quite sure he understood. There would be eyebrows raised, shoulder shrugging. Men would stand together in little groups and talk and women would run from house to house talking, talking. O, the merry little shoulder shruggers! O, the merry little talkers! Where did a man come out in all this? What, in the end, did he think of himself?

There was Natalie, walking along, in the half darkness. She breathed. She was a woman with a body, with arms, legs. She had a trunk to her body and perched upon her neck was a head within which there was a brain. She thought thoughts. She had dreams.

Natalie was walking along a street in the darkness. Her footsteps were ringing out sharp and clear as she stepped along, on the sidewalk.

What did he know of Natalie?

It might well be that, when he and Natalie really knew each other, when they had together faced the problem of living together— Well, it might be that it wouldn't work at all.

John Webster was walking along the street, in the darkness, on the strip of grass, that in Middle Western towns is between the sidewalk and the roadway. He stumbled and came near falling. What was the matter with him? Was he growing tired again?

Did doubts come because he was growing tired? It might well be that everything that had happened to him, during the night, had happened because he was caught up and carried along by a kind of temporary insanity.

What would happen when the insanity had passed, when he became again a sane, a well, a normal man?

Hito, tito, what was the use thinking of turning back when it was too late to turn back? If, in the end, he and Natalie found they could not live together there was still life.

Life was life.   One might still find a way to live a life.

John Webster began to grow courageous again. He looked toward the dark houses along the street and smiled.   He became like a child, playing a game with his fellows of the Wisconsin town.   In the game he was some kind of public character, who because of some brave deed was receiving the applause of the people who lived in the houses.   He imagined himself as riding through the street in a carriage.   The people were sticking their heads out of the windows of the houses and shouting, and he was turning his head from side to side, bowing and smiling.

As Natalie was not looking he enjoyed himself for a moment, playing the game.   As he walked along he kept turning his head from side to side and bowing.   There was a rather absurd smile on his lips.

The old Harry!

"Chinaberries grow on a chinaberry tree!"

All the same it would be better if Natalie did not make such a racket with her feet walking on stone and brick sidewalks.

One might be found out.   It might be that, quite suddenly, without any warning, all the people, now sleeping so peacefully in the dark houses along the street, would sit up in their beds and begin to laugh. That would be terrible and it would be just the sort of thing John Webster would himself do, were he a respectable man in bed with a lawfully wedded wife, and saw some other man doing some such fool thing as he was now doing.*

It was annoying. The night was warm but John Webster felt somewhat cold. He shivered. It was no doubt due to the fact that he was tired. Perhaps thinking of the respectable married people lying in beds in the houses, between which he and Natalie were passing, had made him shiver. One could be very cold, being a respectable married man and lying in bed with a respectable wife. A thought that had been coming and going in his mind for two weeks now came again: "Perhaps I am insane and have infected Natalie, and for that matter my daughter Jane too, with my insanity."

There was no use crying over spilled milk. "What's the use thinking about the matter now?"

"Diddle de di do!"

"Chinaberries grow on a chinaberry tree!"

He and Natalie had come out of the section of town where working people lived and were now passing before houses in which lived merchants, small manufacturers, such men as John Webster had himself been, lawyers, doctors, and such fellows too. Now they were passing the house in which his own banker lived. "The stingy cuss. He has plenty of money. Why doesn't he build himself a larger and finer house?"

To the east, dimly seen through trees and above tree tops, there was a light place coming into the sky.

Now they had come to a place where there were several vacant lots. Some one had given the lots to the town and there was a movement on foot to raise money with which to build a public library. A man had come to John Webster to ask him to contribute to a fund for the purpose. That was but a few days ago.

He had enjoyed the situation immensely. Now he felt like giggling over the remembrance of it.

He had been seated, and as he thought, looking very dignified, at his desk in the factory office when the man came in and told him of the plan. A desire to make an ironic gesture had taken possession of him.

"I am making rather elaborate plans about that fund and my contributing to it but do not want to say what I am planning to do at this particular moment," he had announced. What a falsehood! The matter had not interested him in the least. He had simply enjoyed the man's surprise at his unexpected interest and was having a good time making a swaggering gesture.

The man who came to see him had once served with him on a committee of the Chamber of Commerce, a committee appointed to make an effort to bring new industries into the town.

"I didn't know you were specially interested in literary matters," the man had said.

A troop of derisive thoughts had popped into John Webster's head.

"O, you would be surprised," he had assured the man. At the moment he had felt as he fancied a terrier might feel as it worried a rat.

"I think American literary men have done wonders to uplift the people," he had said, very solemnly. "Why, do you realize that it is our writers who have kept us constantly reminded of the moral code and of the virtues? Such men as you and I, who own factories and who are in a way responsible for the happiness and welfare of the people of the community, cannot be too grateful to our American literary men. I'll tell you what, they are really such strong, red-blooded fellows, always standing up for the right."

John Webster laughed at the thought of his talk with the man from the Chamber of Commerce and at the remembrance of the confused look in the man's eyes as he went away.

Now, as he and Natalie walked along, the intersecting streets led away to the east. There was no doubt a new day was coming. He stopped to light a match and look at his watch. They would be just in comfortable time for the train. Soon now they would be coming into the business section of town where they would both have to make a clattering noise as they walked on stone pavements, but then it would not matter. People did not sleep in the business sections of towns.

He wished it were possible for him to speak to Natalie, to ask her to walk on the grass and not to awaken the people sleeping in the houses. "Well, I'm going to do it," he thought. It was odd how much courage it took now just to speak to her. Neither of them had spoken since they had set out

261

together on this adventure. He stopped and stood for a moment and Natalie, realizing that he was no longer walking beside her, also stopped.

"What is it? What's the matter, John?" she asked. It was the first time she had addressed him by that name. It made everything easier, her having done that.

Still his throat was a little tight. It couldn't be that he also wanted to weep. What nonsense.

There was no need accepting defeat with Natalie until defeat came. There were two sides to this matter of his passing judgment on what he had done. To be sure there was a chance, a possibility, that he had made all this row, upset all his past life, made a mess of things for his wife and daughter, and for Natalie too, to no purpose, merely because he had wanted to escape the boredom of his past existence.

He stood on the strip of grass at the edge of a lawn before a silent respectable house, some one's home. He was trying to see Natalie clearly, trying to see himself clearly. What kind of a figure was he cutting? The light was not very clear. Natalie was but a dark mass before him. His own thoughts were but a dark mass before him.

"Am I just a lustful man wanting a new woman?" he asked himself.

Suppose that were true. What did it mean?

"I am myself. I am trying to be myself," he told himself stoutly.

One should try to live outside oneself too, to live

in others. Had he tried to live in Natalie? He had gone within Natalie. Had he gone within her because there was something within her the had wanted and needed, something he loved?

There was something within Natalie that had set fire to something within himself. It was that ability in her to set him afire he had wanted, still wanted.

She had done that for him, was still doing it for him. When he could no longer respond to her he could perhaps find other loves. She could do that too.

He laughed softly. There was a kind of gladness in him now. He had made of himself, and of Natalie too, what is called disreputable characters. Back into his fancy came a troop of figures, all in their own ways disreputable characters. There was the white-haired old man he had once seen walking with a certain air of being proud and glad of the road, an actress he had seen coming out at the stage entrance of a theatre, a sailor who had thrown his bag aboard a ship and had walked off along a street with a certain air of being proud and glad of the life within himself.

There were such fellows in the world.

The fanciful picture in John Webster's mind changed. There was a certain man going into a room. He had closed the door. A row of candles stood on a mantle above a fireplace. The fellow was playing some kind of game with himself. Well, every one played some kind of game with himself. The fellow in the picture of his fancy had taken a silver crown out of a box. He had put it on his head. "I crown myself with the crown of life," he said.

Was it a silly performance? If it was, what did that matter?

He took a step toward Natalie and then stopped again. "Come woman, walk on the grass. Don't make such a row as we go along," he said aloud.

Now he was walking with a certain swagger toward Natalie who stood in silence at the edge of the sidewalk waiting for him. He went and stood before her and looked into her face. It was true she had been weeping. Even in the faint light there were traces of tears to be seen on her cheeks. "I only had a silly notion. I didn't want to disturb anyone as we went away," he said, laughing softly again. He put his hand on her arm and drew her toward him and they went on again, both now stepping softly and gingerly on the grass between the sidewalk and the roadway.

TEXTUAL NOTES

The abbreviations used in the textual notes are as follows:

D =   The Dial version of the novel published serially from October 1922 through March 1923.

H =   The first book-form printing of the novel by Ben Huebsch in February 1923.

MS =   148-page typewritten manuscript (housed at the Newberry Library) with notes by SA and the printer, and red pencil marks by J.D.C. who reported on the manuscript to its purchaser, Mr. Burton Emmett, on 24 June 1929. Appears to be fair copy of The Dial magazine version.

MS₁ =   168-page manuscript consisting of pages and partial pages of pica and elite typing and galley sheets, and with editorial notes by both SA and the printer. Appears to be the fair copy for the Huebsch edition.

SA =   Sherwood Anderson.

Note: the first number indicates page; the second number, line.

6:4   After the word "Well" no comma appears in either MS (p. 5) or D (p. 364).

7:27   MS (p. 6) and D (p. 365) read: "She had never spoken to him before in just that way." In MS₁ "in" is changed to "with" and "way" to "manner."

8:9   Spelled "judgement" in MS (p. 6) and D (p. 365).

9:21   MS (p. 7) and D (p. 366) omit seven paragraphs from 9:21 through 12:10.

10:4   SA punctuates with a period, not an exclamation point in MS_1 (p. 11).

11:4   SA punctuates with a period, not an exclamation point in MS_1 (p. 11).

12:14   MS (p. 7) reads: "strange joyous things now."

13:29   In D (p. 367) "that" reads "which." In MS (p. 8) "that" is typed and crossed out and "which" is written above. SA changes "which" to "that" in MS_1 (p. 14).

14:1   In MS (p. 8) and D (p. 367) "oneself" reads "himself"; the word is changed to "oneself" in MS_1 (p. 14).

14:19   MS (p. 9) and D (p. 367) omit 14:19 through 14:27 and read: "A rhythm of thought went on within him. 'There must be more than one of me....'" In a typed marginal note in MS_1 (p. 14) SA adds: "that was in some way ... to say strange words."

16:14   MS (p. 10) reads: "That would explain many things if it had happened."

17:2   MS (p. 10) and D (p. 368) conclude Book I with this sentence and omit 17:3 through 17:28.

18:14   MS (p. 11) and D (p. 369) read: "sitting up and dropping a book she had been reading on the grass at his feet."

18:22   "dullness" is correctly typed in MS, but the second "l" is crossed out in pencil. D (p. 369) spells the word "dulness" and repeats the error in the following paragraph.

19:14   MS (p. 11) and D (p. 369) omit 19:15 through 20:4.

19:15   In MS_1 (p. 18) SA typed "in the hammock at his daughter's feet"; "at his daughter's feet" is crossed out in green ink.

19:16 In MS (p. 11) the sentence concludes: "and he took that up and read a few lines"; "that" is crossed out in green ink, and above it the word "it" is written.

19:16 In MS$_1$ (p. 18) SA typed two additional lines which are crossed out in green ink: "Umbrage threw out his hands with a gesture of despair. 'It is a great loss,' he said, 'a very decided mistake.'"

20:14 In MS (p. 11) and D (p. 369) SA uses the word "estate" instead of "state."

20:18 In MS (p. 11) and D (p. 369) SA writes: "Her face was like a fair sheet of paper on which nothing had been written." By placing the sentence in quotation marks and changing the verb tenses to present and present perfect, respectively, SA renders the sentence a directly articulated thought of John Webster's.

20:19 In MS (p. 12) and D (pp. 369-370) lines 20:19 through 20:25 are a continuation of the paragraph beginning with line 20:5, not a separate paragraph.

20:19 MS (p. 12) and D (p. 369) read: "Her eyes in wandering about met his eyes."

21:24 Spelled "colourless" in D (p. 370) and MS (p. 12).

21:29 D (p. 370) misprints "tower" as "flower."

22:15 MS (p. 13) and D (p. 371) omit the comma after "town."

23:28 MS (p. 14) and D (p. 371) use the singular "breast."

24:18 Book II of MS (p. 14) and D (p. 372) concludes with the sentence: "The window of his room was open and a breeze blew in and across his body." Sentences 24:18 through 25:7 are omitted.

27:3 MS (p. 15) and D (p. 372) read: "Nothing can be beautiful that is not loved." In MS$_1$ (p. 22) SA prints "either animate or inanimate" in blue ink.

27:15 No comma in MS (p. 15) or D (p. 373); comma added in green ink in MS$_1$ (p. 23).

27:20   Spelled "neighbours" in MS (p. 16) and D (p. 373).

28:28   MS (p. 16) and D (p. 374) read: "in which he walked."

29:12   The word "perhaps" is not capitalized in MS (p. 17)
        or D (p. 374).

29:12   In MS (p. 17) the "ve" in "have" is pencilled out to
        read "had."

30:3   No comma after "eyes" in MS (p. 17) or D (p. 374).

31:12   SA expanded this paragraph in H. MS (p. 18) and D
        (p. 375) read: "Her name was Katherine and her
        coming to work for the Websters long ago had brought
        on a quarrel between John Webster and his wife. A
        young man of Indianapolis, who worked in a bank, had
        stolen a large sum of money and had run away with a
        woman who was a servant in his father's house. He
        had been killed in the wreck as he sat with the woman
        and all trace of him had been lost until someone from
        Indianapolis, quite by chance, saw and recognized
        Katherine on the streets of her adopted town. The
        question asked was, what had become of the stolen
        money, and Katherine had been accused of knowing
        and of concealing it."

31:13   D (p. 375) omits the period after "Mrs".

32:21   MS (p. 19) and D (p. 376) omit 32:14 through 32:21.
        SA adds the two paragraphs in a type-written note in
        MS$_1$ (p. 26).

32:29   Spelled "splendour" in MS (p. 19) and D (p. 376).

33:5   No comma after "day" in MS (p. 19) and D (p. 376).

34:10   MS (p. 20) and D (p. 377) read: "As for the stolen
        money..."

34:14   MS (p. 20) and D (p. 377) read: "... the crime was
        put upon him." SA crosses out "him" and writes
        "her lover" in green ink in the margin of MS$_1$ (p. 27).

34:16   MS (p. 20) and D (p. 377) read: "... in that bank
        ..." SA crosses out "that" and writes "the" in black
        ink in the margin of MS$_1$ (p. 27).

35:7   In MS$_1$ (p. 27) SA first typed "that," then crossed it out and wrote "her" above, and finally crossed out "her" and wrote "Katherine."

35:10   MS (pp. 20-21) and D (p. 377) omit 34:20 through 35:10.

35:15   Spelled "colour" in MS (p. 21) and D (p. 377).

35:16   MS (p. 21) and D (p. 377) omit 35:17 through 35:31.

36:5   MS (p. 21) and D (p. 377) read: "Tomorrow perhaps things would be different." In MS$_1$ (p. 28) "perhaps" is crossed out in black ink.

36:18   MS (p. 21) and D (p. 377) read: "He was some kind of professor ..." In MS$_1$ (p. 28) "some kind of" is crossed out in green ink.

38:1   MS (p. 22) and D (p. 378) read: "... clean your house." In MS$_1$ (p. 29) the letters "se" are added in black ink, thus changing the word "clean" to "cleanse."

39:11   MS (p. 22) and D (p. 378) omit 38:2 through 39:11.

39:17   MS (p. 22) and D (p. 378) read: "... that frightened one." In MS$_1$ (p. 30) "one" is crossed out and "him" written in green ink above it.

40:5   MS (p. 23) reads: "Anyway now ..."

41:6   MS (p. 24) and D (p. 379) read: "... said a little prayer of some kind." In MS$_1$ (p. 31) "of some kind" is crossed out in green ink.

41:20   MS (p. 24) and D (p. 380) read: "... too much absorbed in his affairs to be aware." In MS$_1$ (p. 32) SA inked in "own trivial" in the margin with an arrow placing the words between "his" and "affairs."

41:26   A period, rather than an exclamation point, concludes this sentence in MS (p. 24), D (p. 380), and MS$_1$ (p. 32).

42:3   MS (p. 24) and D (p. 380) read: "... of his own body ..." In MS$_1$ (p. 32) "his" is crossed out and "one's" is printed above in green ink.

42:4   A period rather than a question mark concludes the sentence in MS (p. 24), D (p. 380), and MS_1 (p. 32).

42:4   MS (p. 24) and D (p. 380) read: "... of his own body ..." In MS_1 (p. 32) "His" is crossed out and "one's" is printed above in green ink.

42:20   MS (p. 25) and D (p. 380) omit lines 42:11 through 42:20. MS_1 (p. 32) consists of part of a galley sheet from D (p. 380 1-20) and a typed note containing the two additional paragraphs.

42:22   MS (p. 25) and D (p. 380) read: "... not get himself out of ..." In MS_1 (p. 33) the letters "him" are crossed out and "one" printed above in green ink.

42:23   MS (p. 25) and D (p. 380) read: "He went and sat on a bench in a little park in the very centre of his town and began trying to think along another road." In MS_1 (p. 33) "went and sat on a bench in a little park in the very centre of his town and" is crossed out in green ink.

42:26   MS (p. 25) and D (p. 380) use the plural "grape-fruits"; the "s" is crossed out in MS_1 (p. 33).

43:5   Spelled "colour" in MS (p. 25) and D (p. 380).

43:21   MS (p. 25) reads: "How filled with fragrant suggestive smells life might be, for example." D (p. 381) omits "for example." In MS, D, and MS_1 (p. 34) the sentence ends with a period, not an exclamation point.

44:3   MS (p. 26) and D (p. 381) read: "... at just this time of the year, for one thing, farmers ..." The words "for one thing" are crossed out in MS_1 (p. 34).

44:6   MS (p. 26), D (p. 381), and MS_1 (p. 34) read: "... everyone had great cellers under their houses ..."

44:8   MS (p. 26) and D (p. 381) read "... apples, turnips, and such things." In MS_1 (p. 34) "and such things" is crossed out and a period placed after "turnips."

44:8   MS (p. 26) and D (p. 381) read: "There was a thing man had learned to do." In MS$_1$ (p. 34) "thing" and "to do" are crossed out and "trick" is substituted for "thing."

44:10   MS (p. 26) and D (p. 381) read: "... near the town and many things, pumpkins, squashes, heads of ..." The words "many things" are crossed out in MS$_1$ (p. 34).

44:17   MS (p. 26) and D (p. 381) read: "Wagons arrived bringing things to his father's house." In MS$_1$ (p. 34) "bringing things to" is crossed out and "at" printed above in green ink.

44:19   Spelled "grey" in MS (p. 26) and D (p. 381).

44:26   Spelled "parlour" in MS (p. 26) and D (p. 381).

45:20   MS (p. 27) and D (p. 382) read: "... one had gone upstairs and got into ..." The word "had" is added in green ink in MS$_1$ (p. 35).

45:21   MS (p. 27) and D (p. 382) read: "... farm men who had brought the things." The words "who had brought the things" are crossed out in MS$_1$ (p. 35).

45:25   Spelled "grey" in MS (p. 27) and D (p. 382).

45:25   MS (p. 27) and D (p. 382) read: "... the grey horse along the street ..." The word "off" is inserted in green ink in MS$_1$ (p. 35).

46:1   Spelled "grey" in MS (p. 27) and D (p. 382).

46:10   Spelled "grey" in MS (p. 28) and D (p. 382).

46:12   The word "tucked," used in MS (p. 28) and D (p. 382), is changed to "stored" in MS$_1$ (p. 35).

46:13   The section serialized in the October 1922 issue of D ends here.

47:7   Spelled "greyness" in MS (p. 29) and D (p. 533).

47:14   MS (p. 29) and D (p. 533) read: "... and laughed swiftly ..." In MS$_1$ (p. 36) "swiftly" is crossed out in black ink and "softly" printed in the margin.

48:11   MS (p. 29) and D (p. 533) read: "He had explained the matter to the banker." In MS_1 (p. 36) "He" is crossed out in green ink and "The manufacturer had become self-conscious and" is printed in the left margin.

49:8   MS (p. 30) reads: "Other men had got into that position through the power of advertising." A pencilled revision in MS_1 (p. 37) is incorporated in D to read: "... into a position like that through the power of ..."

49:9   D (p. 534) reads: "Why shouldn't he do the same?"

49:21   MS (p. 30) reads: "It was odd." In MS_1 (p. 37) "odd" is crossed out and "amazing" printed in black ink in the right margin. D (p. 534) reads: "It was amazing."

50:8   D (p. 534) omits "He began to scold himself" and asks instead, "Would he never grow up?"

51:14   MS (p. 31) and D (p. 534) omit 50:9 through 51:14. The two paragraphs are added in MS_1 (pp. 38-39).

51:25   MS (p. 31) reads: "now the river was low and a little stream of water ran through the wide banks of caked mud." In MS_1 (p. 39) "a little stream" is crossed out and "only a narrow channel" is printed in green ink above. D (p. 535) incorporates the revision.

52:10   Spelled without a hyphen in MS (p. 32).

52:22   MS (p. 32) concludes the paragraph and Book IV: "He suddenly felt very resolute and strong." D (p. 535) concludes at the same point but omits "suddenly."

53:5   MS (p. 32) and D (p. 535) omit 52:23 through 53:5. The two paragraphs are added in a typed note in MS_1 (p. 40).

54:19   MS (p. 33) and D (p. 536) read: "An amazing thing had happened." In MS_1 (p. 41) "and lovely" is added after "amazing."

55:6   MS (p. 33) reads: "... to Chicago and then that was all as by a quick miracle, swept away." In MS_1 (p. 41) "that" is crossed out and "the mud and dirt" written beneath in black ink. D (p. 536) incorporates the revision.

55:15   MS (p. 34), D (p. 536), and MS_1 (p. 41) read: "He remembered to have seen her come in with it wrapped in a paper package."

56:15   MS (p. 34) reads: "... had provided herself a bottle of whiskey." In MS_1 (p. 41) the word "with" is inserted in black ink. D (p. 537) incorporates the revision.

56:21   MS (p. 34) reads: "'What is Natalie up to,'"; D (p. 537) italicizes "is" and punctuates the sentence with a question mark.

56:28   MS (p. 35) uses the word "him"; this is changed to "himself" in MS_1 (p. 42) and incorporated in D (p. 537).

57:11   MS (p. 35) uses the singular, "thought."

57:18   MS (p. 35) reads "... crying to one another" which is changed to "crying to each other" in MS_1 (p. 42) and incorporated in D (p. 537).

58:13   MS (p. 36) and D (p. 538) read: "The cleansing thing was going on and ..."

58:25   MS (p. 36) reads "... a light suspended ..." In MS_1 (p. 43) "light" is crossed out and "lamp" written in black ink in the right margin. D (p. 538) incorporates the revision.

59:8   The sentence in MS (p. 37) begins with "Then," omitted in D (p. 538). Lines 59:6 through 59:8 conclude the paragraph beginning on 58:32 in D.

59:13   MS (p. 37) and D (p. 538) read: "... while the other two women went to the left." In MS_1 (p. 44) "women" is crossed out in black ink.

59:14   In MS (p. 37) and D (p. 538) the sentence reads: "The book-keeper and the older of the women did not speak of what they had all seen." Revision is completed in green and in black ink in MS$_1$ (p. 44).

59:21 MS (p. 37) reads: "... businesses go to pieces."
In MS (p. 44) the letters "es" and the word "go" are
crossed out in black ink. The word "goes" is written
in the left margin.

59:31 MS (p. 38) and D (p. 539) read: "The youngest of
the three women, ..." The word "women" is crossed
out in black ink in MS1 (p. 59).

60:17 MS (p. 38) reads: "... after a little ..." In MS$_1$
(p. 44) "little" is crossed out in black ink, and "time"
is printed in the left margin.

60:18 MS (p. 38) reads: "... no one near her, ..."
MS$_1$ (p. 44) strikes "her," and D (p. 539) incorporates
the deletion.

63:9 Spelled "neighbour" in MS (pp. 39-40) and D (p. 539).

63:10 MS (pp. 39-40) and D (p. 539) read: "... late afternoon he was always to be seen ..." The word "he"
is crossed out and "the German" is printed above in
green ink in MS1 (p. 45).

64:2 Punctuation varies. In MS (pp. 39-40) SA wrote two
sentences: "There were three doors. One leading
into a hallway, one into the room where his wife
slept, and a third that led into his daughter's room."
D (p. 540) combines the sentences: "There were
three doors, one leading ... his daughter's room."

64:22 MS (p. 41) and D (p. 541) read: "... should not cohabit except for ..." In MS1 (p. 46) SA crossed out
"cohabit" and printed "be lovers" in green ink in the
right margin.

65:4 Misspelled "ecstacy" in MS (p. 41).

65:10 MS (p. 41) reads: "... and to his fellow men." In
MS$_1$ (p. 46) "his" is crossed out and "one's" written
in black ink in the left margin.

67:3 SA uses instead the contraction "didn't" in MS (p. 43)
and D (p. 542). He revised to "did not" in MS1 (p.
47).

67:11   MS (p. 43) and D (p. 542) read: "... but they did not think of eating." In MS$_1$ (p. 47) "they" is crossed out and "the man and woman" printed in black ink in the right margin.

67:16   MS (p. 43) and D (p. 542) read: "... romantic figures to him." In MS$_1$ (p. 47) "to him" is crossed out and "in his awakening mind" is printed in black ink.

67:30   MS (p. 43) reads: "He had been something like this sometimes when he was a boy, but no one then had ever understood the riotous play of his fancy and in time he had come to think letting his fancy go all foolishness." SA revised in MS$_1$ (p. 47), and D (p. 542) incorporates the revision.

67:32   In MS (p. 43) and MS$_1$ (p. 47) the word "flare-up" is not hyphenated.

68:20   MS (p. 44) and D (p. 543) include the following paragraph which is crossed out in MS$_1$ (p. 48) and omitted in H: "For every woman there is a lover and when there are not enough lovers to go around two or three of the women sometimes have the same lover or its the other way about. It all depends, you see, on how much love the man or woman is capable of feeling. That's all that counts in this street."

69:12   In MS (p. 44) SA used "I shall" rather than the contraction "I'll." Revised in MS$_1$ (p. 48) and incorporated in D (p. 543).

69:13   In MS (p. 44) SA used "I will" rather than "I'll." Revised in MS (p. 48) and incorporated in D (p. 543).

69:14   MS (p. 44) reads: "... the entire ownership ..." The word "entire" is crossed out in MS$_1$ (p. 48). D (p. 543) incorporates the deletion.

71:28   Spelled "neighbours" in MS (p. 46) and D (p. 545).

72:24   SA revised the "himself" from MS (p. 47) to "oneself" in MS$_1$ (p. 50).

74:24   MS (p. 48) reads: "... and it was the same with the two older of the women employees in the office." In

MS$_1$ (p. 51) the words "of the" and "employees" are crossed out, and D (p. 546) incorporates the deletion.

75:1 MS (p. 48) reads: "... younger of the three women still ..." The word "women" is crossed out in MS$_1$ (p. 51) and deleted in D (p. 546).

76:13 MS (p. 49) reads: "The walls of the houses had receded away from them." In MS$_1$ (p. 51) the word "away" is crossed out. D (p. 547) deletes the "from them" and reads: "The walls of the houses had receded."

76:16 MS (p. 49) and D (p. 547) read: "... and the walls of the house had fallen down." In MS$_1$ (p. 52) SA made "walls" singular and printed the word "front" in black ink.

76:23 MS (p. 49) uses the word "and," not "or." SA revised in MS$_1$ (p. 53).

78:8 The word "wind," not "sheet," is used in MS (p. 51). SA revised in MS$_1$ (p. 53).

78:27 The November 1922 installment of The Dial concludes here.

79:7 MS (p. 51) reads: "... not now very happy hours." The word "hours" is crossed out in MS (p. 54) and deleted in D (p. 623).

79:14 SA used the singular "sprout" in MS (p. 51) and pluralized in MS$_1$ (p. 54).

79:21 MS (p. 51) reads: "... a letter came in she ..." The word "in" is crossed out in MS$_1$ (p. 54) and deleted in D (p. 623).

79:26 SA uses "will" rather than "shall" in MS (p. 79).

80:10 MS (p. 52) reads: "... along the dark railroad tracks ..." The word "dark" is crossed out in MS$_1$ (p. 55) and deleted in D (p. 625).

81:25 MS (p. 53) reads: "Natalie and all the others except the younger of the two women had gone out." In MS$_1$ (p. 55) the words "younger" and "two" are changed to "youngest" and "three," respectively.

81:28   MS (p. 53) reads: "... thoughts and feelings that they had none of them wanted to stay there when they were not working." In MS$_1$ (p. 55) "They had" is crossed out in black ink.

82:5   In MS (p. 53) and D (p. 625) spelled "grey." Spelling is changed in pencil in MS$_1$ (p. 55).

82:12   MS (p. 54) reads: "'It would be dreadful if she would try to speak about it,' he thought and then at once, for some unexplainable reason, knew she would not try to do that." In MS$_1$ "would" is crossed out in black ink and changed to "should." D (p. 626) reads: "... knew she would not try that."

83:23   MS (p. 55) reads: "... not unlike Natalie sometimes looked." The words "sometimes looked" are crossed out in black ink in MS$_1$ (p. 56).

84:15   In MS (p. 55) and D (p. 626) spelled "colour." The "u" is pencilled out in MS$_1$ (p. 57).

84:25   MS (p. 55) reads: "I will tell Natalie of that tonight and I will tell her also of what I intend to do at home there in my room. I will tell her and she will say nothing." In MS$_1$ (p. 57) SA changed "will" to "shall."

89:20   In MS (p. 59) and D (p. 629), spelled "splendour."

94:2   MS (p. 61) reads: "It came the thing he wanted." In MS$_1$ (p. 61) the words "thing he wanted" are crossed out in black ink and the phrase "sound for which he was listening" is printed above.

94:27   MS (p. 62) and D (p. 631) read: "'I'll talk to mother and sister myself and I'll be waiting for you,' ..." The words "I'll talk to mother and sister myself and" are crossed out in MS$_1$ (p. 62).

95:21   MS (p. 62) reads: "'Hito Tito' ..." SA added the comma and decapitalized "Tito" in MS$_1$ (p. 62).

95:28   Lines 95:18 through 95:28 are omitted in D.

97:12 MS (p. 64) reads: "... that the food given the child did not nourish it, and they were unable to find the right food." In MS$_1$ (p. 63) the words "were unable to ... out" are crossed out and "could not" is printed in the right margin.

97:23 MS (p. 64) reads: "... they have been living ..." In MS$_1$ (p. 63) "have" is inked out and "had" is printed in the right margin.

97:27 MS (p. 64) and D (p. 633) read: "She had rather slender hips, like a boy's hips, but her shoulders were broad." SA changed the sentence to read as it appears in H in MS$_1$ (p. 64).

97:32 MS (p. 64) and D (p. 633) begin the sentence with "Perhaps," but the word is crossed out in MS$_1$ (p. 64).

98:14 MS (p. 65) reads: "... what I'm after here,' ..." In MS$_1$ (p. 64) "here" is crossed out and "now" is printed in the right margin.

98:24 MS (p. 65) reads: "... could warm that out of her." In MS$_1$ (p. 64) "that" is crossed out and "the fear" is printed in the right margin.

99:30 MS (p. 66) reads: "... the scene in the room that he had planned so carefully was going to be a harder matter to handle than he had thought." D (p. 634) reads: "the scene in the room, the talk with his daughter that he had planned so carefully was going to be a harder matter to handle than he had thought." In MS$_1$ (p. 65) "the talk with his daughter" is added in blue ink and the word "thought" is crossed out with "counted on" printed below.

104:26 MS (p. 69) and D (p. 637) read: "... she wanted to hear the story now." In MS$_1$ (p. 68), "the story" is crossed out and "it" is printed in the right margin.

108:14 MS (p. 72) and D (p. 639) do not include "into the clothes he had come to feel had no meaning and were altogether unlovely because the unknown hands that had fashioned them were unmoved by the desire to create beauty." SA added these words in black ink in the bottom margin of MS$_1$ (p. 70).

108:21   MS (p. 72) and D (p. 639) read "his daughter Jane had done a quite lovely thing. There was a certain garment that had to be put on and buttoned. While he did that she turned and threw herself ..." In MS$_1$ (p. 71) SA changed the paragraph to read as it appears in H.

112:10   MS (p. 75) and D (p. 641) read: "... and by something a little strange in the way I had told him." In MS$_1$ (p. 72) "way" is crossed out and "manner in which" is printed in the right margin.

112:14   MS (p. 75) and D (p. 642) read: "being taken that way by something ..." In MS$_1$ (p. 72) "that way" is crossed out and "in that spirit" is printed in the right margin.

116:10   The section serialized in the December 1922 issue of The Dial concludes here.

117:24   MS (p. 79) reads "while" rather than "when," which is written in black ink above the crossed out "while" in MS$_1$ (p. 75).

118:12   MS (p. 79) reads: "... and speak of the matter more in the modern spirit as he himself might have done laughingly, later, one might say ..." SA changed position of "later" in the sentence in MS$_1$ (p. 75).

119:2   MS (p. 80) reads: "He had got out the small bag into which he put the things he might need as he thought of them." In MS$_1$ (p. 75) SA restructured the sentence to read as it appears in H.

123:8   In MS (p. 83), MS$_1$ (p. 78), and D (p. 34), spelled "splendour."

125:9   MS (p. 84) and D (p. 36) use "stay" rather than "wait" which is printed in the right margin of MS$_1$ (p. 80).

126:5   Punctuation of this sentence in MS (p. 85), MS$_1$ (pp. 80-81), and D (p. 36) differs from H: "The devil, he had counted on finding in her the something, well what was it? the something a young fellow is always dreaming of finding in some strange woman ..."

126:9   Printer's error in H: "understand."

127:11   In MS (p. 86), MS₁ (p. 82), and D (p. 37), spelled "colours."

127:13   In MS (p. 86), MS₁ (p. 82), and D (p. 37) spelled "splendours."

128:23   In MS (p. 87) the paragraph continues: "In the kitchen, above the kitchen stove, before which my mother or our servant Adaline was always standing when the house was alive and not dead as it was now, just up there, where one could see it over the women's heads, there was a small clock and now that clock began making a sound as loud as though someone were beating on sheets of iron with big hammers. In the house next door someone was talking steadily or maybe reading aloud. The wife of the man who lived in the next house had been ill in bed for months and perhaps now he was trying to entertain her by reading some story. The words came steadily, but in a broken way too. What I mean is, that there would be a steady little run of sounds, then it would be broken and then begin again. Sometimes the voice would be raised a little, for emphasis no doubt, and that was like a kind of splash, as when the waves along a beach all, for a long time, run to the same place clearly marked on the wet sand and then there comes one wave that goes far beyond all the others and splashes against the face of a rock."

130:4   Lines 128:24 through 130:4 appear in MS₁ (pp. 83-85) and H, but not in MS or D.

130:11   MS (pp. 87-88) and D (p. 38) read: "The voice from the distance was like a voice coming from some hidden buried place in myself." In MS₁ (p. 85) SA pluralized voice, changed "was" to "were," and added "from the German's house next door" in blue ink in the left margin.

135:1   MS (p. 91) and D (p. 41) read: "... I quite calmly got my overcoat and my bag." In MS₁ (p. 87) the

words "my hat" are added to the sentence and printed
in blue ink in the right margin.

136:20   In MS (p. 92) SA used the contraction "didn't" rather
than "did not."

137:18   D (p. 42) concludes the paragraph: "He smiled
gaily. He began to talk." M (p. 93) concludes:
"He smiled gaily. He began to talk, to preach to
her." SA followed with four paragraphs that appear
in MS (pp. 93-94) only:
" 'One denies the body and its functions. All of us
seem to take a great delight in doing that. What
started us all doing it I don't know, but I am sure
I in some way got the notion from my father and
that he got it from his father and that the roots of
the thing go back and back to God knows what source.
Well you see one eats food. It is taken in through
the mouth and goes gaily on its way down through
the body. What I suppose is, that as it goes on its
way, there is a good deal of switching of parts of
it here and there to various organs of the body.
One might have the fancy you see, that eating a
meal of food is a good deal like loading a train.
The meal is eaten. Very well. Let's say the train
is made up and loaded. There is a car for Mem-
phis, Tennessee, one for Kalamazoo in Michigan,
another for Syracuse, New York. The food goes
splashing down the gullet, just as the train goes
rambling off along its tracks.
'But gracious sakes, Jane, it doesn't all go to one
place. That's pretty clear. Well, I am perhaps
rude to try to describe your own slender young body
as a railroad train. A railroad train is such a
noisy rumbling affair after all.
'What I suppose I am trying to say to you is that
in a young man, as in a young woman like yourself,
the life of the body, that is kept going by the eating
of food, and is renewed and rested each night by
sleep, is a thing modern people, like you are now
and I have been until just recently, it is a thing I
say, that we have all taken a great notion to deny
exists. There are the arms, legs, brains, heart,
organs of procreation, organs of digestion, and God
knows what other organs packed away in the human
frame and all trying to do their job and we go about
trying to deny the existence of most of them and the

abuse we give some of them, when you come to
think of the matter, is a living shame.'
He began to laugh at his own seriousness. 'Hito,
Tito, quit your preaching,' he said to himself.''

138:25   In MS (p. 94) and D (p. 42) spelled ''grey.''

141:10   In MS (p. 96), MS$_1$ (p. 90), and D (p. 44) spelled
''colour.''

142:24   The word ''purple'' does not appear in MS (p. 97)
and is penned in blue ink in MS$_1$ (p. 91).

144:11   MS and D omit lines 143:30 through 144:11.

148:9   MS (p. 101) and D (p. 47) read: ''... that just beneath the surface of the ordinary everyday life
about there was deep and ...'' In MS$_1$ (p. 94) the
words ''the'' and ''about'' are inked out to provide the
reading found in H.

148:19   In MS (p. 101) and D (p. 48), SA uses the past
tense ''sat.''

148:28   The punctuation differs in MS (p. 102) and D (p. 48):
''... painted a canvas, an old chair set in an empty
room.''

150:32   In MS (p. 103) and D (p. 49), spelled ''splendour.''
In MS$_1$ (p. 96), the letter ''u'' is pencilled out.

151:15   The section serialized in the January, 1923, issue
of The Dial ends here.

156:27   MS (p. 108) reads: ''Now and when he thought her
gone from the field ...'' In MS$_1$ (p. 100), the words
''Now and'' are inked out.

158:13   Spelled ''grey'' in MS (p. 110) and D (p. 169). The
letter ''e'' is pencilled out and changed to ''a'' in
MS$_1$ (p. 101).

159:2   See note 158:13.

159:4   See note 158:13.

159:12   Spelled ''grey'' in MS (p. 110) and D (p. 169). The letter "e" is pencilled out and changed to "a" in MS$_1$ (p. 102).

159:26   SA uses "would" rather than "could" in MS (p. 110). The "w" is inked out and the letter "c" printed in the right margin of MS$_1$ (p. 102).

160:6   In MS (p. 111), SA uses "trainsmen," rather than "trainmen." In MS$_1$ (p. 102) the letter "s" is pencilled out.

163:24   The paragraph from 163:15 through 163:24 does not appear in MS, MS$_1$, or D.

164:13   In MS (p. 114) the word "Everyone" is bracketed in red pencil, and the words "People everywhere" are pencilled above. MS$_1$ (p. 105) and D (p. 172) read: "Everyone told things ..."

168:7   In MS (p. 117), MS$_1$ (p. 108), and D (p. 174) spelled "colours."

169:18   SA uses "girl" rather than "woman" in MS (p. 118). In MS$_1$ (p. 108), "girl" is crossed out in green ink and "woman" is printed above it.

169:20   The phrase "such a young woman" is printed in the right margin of MS$_1$ (p. 108) and replaces the pronoun "she" used in MS (p. 118).

170:3   The paragraph from 169:30 through 170:3 has the following variant readings:
MS (p. 118): "One went up the stairs and softly into the room where the woman was lying on the bed. One held the lamp above his head. Its light shone into his eyes and into the eyes of the woman.   There was a long slow time when they stood just so, looking at each other."
MS1 (p. 109): "One went up the stairs and softly into the room where the woman was lying on the bed. One held the lamp above one's [the word "his" is crossed out and "one's" printed in the right margin] head.   Its light shone into one's [again, "one's" replaces "his"] eyes and into the eyes of the woman. There was a long slow time when the two [the letter "y" is crossed out in the word "they" and "two" is inked in above; thus, "the two" replaces "they"]

stood so, looking at each other."
D (p. 175): "One went up the stairs and into the
room where the woman was lying on the bed. The
light, held swinging slightly in the quiet air, shone
into the eyes of the woman. There was a long slow
time when the two people looked quietly at each other."

170:29   In MS (p. 119), MS_1 (p. 109), and D (p. 176) spelled
"vapour."

173:2   MS (p. 120) reads: "A lid was jerked off somewhere in me." In MS_1 (p. 111), "something" is
printed in green ink in the right margin.

173:20   The contraction "didn't," used in MS (p. 121) is
changed to "did not" in MS_1 (p. 111).

174:26   In MS (p. 122) the sentence ends "... above her."
The word "her" is crossed out in green ink in MS_1
(p. 112).

176:3   MS (p. 123) reads: "... in respectable Wisconsin
manufacturing towns." "Wisconsin" is crossed out
and "Illinois" is printed in green ink in the right
margin of MS_1 (p. 113).

178:5   MS (p. 124) reads: "A lump came up into his
throat." In MS_1 (p. 114) "up" is crossed out in
green ink.

179:10   MS (p. 125) reads: "One did well enough to have his
own thoughts, straighten out his own matters." The
word "his," used twice in the sentence, is replaced
by "one's" in MS_1 (p. 115).

180:23   In MS (p. 126) and D (p. 182), spelled "odours" and
changed to "odors" in MS_1 (p. 116).

180:26   MS (p. 126) and D (p. 182) read: "... could turn
his fancy loose." The word "his" is crossed out
and "one's" is printed in black in the right margin
of MS_1 (p. 116).

181:20   The section serialized in the February, 1923, issue
of The Dial ends here.

182:8   In MS (p. 127) and D (p. 256), SA uses the pronoun "herself" instead of "the woman." In MS_1 (p. 117) "herself" is crossed out in black ink and "the woman" is printed in the bottom margin.

182:22   MS (p. 128) and D (p. 256) conclude the sentence: "... moving about among the trees." In MS_1 (p. 118) "the" is crossed out in green ink.

184:1   The word "color," used five times in this paragraph, is spelled "colour" in MS (p. 129) and D (p. 257). SA changed the spelling in MS_1 (p. 119).

184:3   MS (p. 129) and D (p. 257) conclude the sentence: "... within me too." In MS_1 (p. 119) "me" is inked out and "myself" printed in the right margin in black ink.

186:6   MS (p. 130) reads: "He had begun to feel mean then." In MS_1 (p. 120) the words "He" and "then" are crossed out in green ink and the phrases "Then he also" and "and unclean" are printed in the right margin.

186:31   This sentence does not appear in MS (p. 131) but is printed in black ink in the right margin of MS_1 (p. 121).

187:13   In MS (p. 131) and D (p. 259) the sentence concludes: "... didn't know." The "n't" is crossed out and "not" printed in black ink in the bottom margin of MS_1 (p. 121).

189:6   MS (p. 132) reads: "What he, at the time thought was that she wasn't a woman after all, but a child." In MS_1 (p. 122) "but" is crossed out in green ink, and "She was" is printed in the right margin.

189:20   In MS (p. 133) and D (p. 260), SA uses the contraction "didn't" rather than "did not." The "n't" is crossed out and "not" printed in black ink in the right margin of MS_1 (p. 123).

189:31   MS (p. 133) reads: "It was rather a puzzling notion, but the truth was, that every time during the last few weeks he had looked at his wife he had wanted to run at once and look at himself in a glass." In

MS$_1$ (p. 123) the position of the phrase "during the last few weeks" is changed so that the sentence is structured as in H.

191:13   MS (p. 134) reads: "The thing to bear in mind now, at this moment, however, was ..." D (p. 261) reads the same as H except for commas following "mind" and "however." The word "however" is crossed out in green ink and repositioned to follow "mind" in MS$_1$ (p. 124).

191:27   In MS (p. 134), SA uses "his" rather than "one's." The pronoun is crossed out and "one's" printed above in green ink in MS$_1$ (p. 124).

191:29   In MS (p. 134) SA uses "her" rather than "the woman." In MS$_1$ (p. 124) "her" is crossed out and "the woman" printed in green ink in the right margin.

192:25   Reads "oneself" in MS$_1$ (p. 125) and D (p. 262).

193:1   Reads "his" in MS (p. 135) and D (p. 262). The pronoun is crossed out and "one's" is printed in black ink in the left margin of MS$_1$ (p. 125).

193:28   The phrase "bobbing its head up too" is printed in black ink in MS$_1$ (p. 126) and does not appear in MS (p. 136).

194:4   In MS (p. 136) the sentence concludes: "... in the room too." The word "too" is crossed out and "same" printed in green ink in the right margin of MS$_1$ (p. 126).

195:19   MS (p. 137) and D (p. 264) read: "... were loading and unloading." The "ing's" are crossed out and "ed" printed in green ink in the right margin of MS$_1$ (p. 127).

196:19   Spelled "colour" in MS (p. 138) and D (p. 265). The "u" is pencilled out in MS$_1$ (p. 128).

198:1   SA uses "for which" here in MS (p. 139) and D (p. 265). The prepositional phrase is crossed out and "and" is printed above in black ink in MS$_1$ (p. 129).

200:12 Spelled "grey" in MS (p. 141) and D (0. 267). The "e" is pencilled out and "a" printed in the right margin of MS$_1$ (p. 130).

200:28 Capitalized "Tito" in MS (p. 141).

201:10 Used twice in this sentence, "colourless" in MS (p. 142) and D (pp. 267-68). The "u's" are pencilled out in MS$_1$ (p. 131).

203:7 Spelled "colour" in MS (p. 143) and D (p. 269). The "u" is pencilled out in MS$_1$ (p. 132).

203:11 Spelled "colour" in MS (p. 143) and D (p. 269). The "u's" are pencilled out in MS$_1$ (p. 133).

204:18 MS (p. 144), MS$_1$ (p. 133), and D (p. 270) read: "thoughts," not "things."

206:4 In MS (p. 146) SA uses "his" rather than "the." The personal pronoun is pencilled out in MS$_1$ (p. 134) and "the" is printed in the bottom margin.

206:8 In MS (p. 146) the sentence begins: "However when he had ..." "However" is pencilled out in MS$_1$ (p. 134).

207:2 The position of "again" is changed in MS$_1$ (p. 135). MS (p. 146) reads: "Now perhaps the lid would never stir from its place again."

207:3 MS (p. 146) uses "in" rather than "on." In MS$_1$ (p. 135) "in" is pencilled out and "on" is printed in the right margin.

207:28 SA uses "them" in MS (p. 147), but the word is pencilled out and "him" is printed in the right margin of MS$_1$ (p. 135).

208:10 "Paradise Lost" is not placed in quotation marks in MS (p. 147) and D (p. 272). Pencilled quotation marks appear in MS$_1$ (p. 136).

208:17 In MS (p. 147) the sentence begins: "All evening perhaps there ..." The word "perhaps" is pencilled out in MS$_1$ (p. 136).

209:4   SA uses the singular "saying" in MS (p. 148). The "s" is added in pencil in MS₁ (p. 136).

209:14   MS (p. 148) and the final section serialized in the March, 1923, issue of The Dial conclude here.

222:31   Pp. 141-43 of MS₁ are missing; thus, there is no extant ms. version of lines 218:27 through 222:31.

222:13   MS₁ (p. 144) reads: "One could not love until they had cleansed and a little beautified their own bodies and minds, until they had opened the doors of their beings and let in sun and air, until they had freed their own mind and fancies."

226:17   MS₁ (p. 146) reads: "It was odd, she now had a sharp and distinct sense of death, in some way connected with her mother's figure."

229:14   SA does not use the possessive form of "horses" in MS₁ (p. 148).

233:7   This sentence does not appear in MS₁ (p. 151).

236:22   MS₁ (p. 154) is brown and faded at this point, but the sentence appears to have ended: "... to a resort called Cedar Point." The word "called" is crossed out and "near" printed above it in blue ink.

237:8   In MS₁ (p. 154) the sentence originally read: "On that day in Sandusky, ..." The words "in Sandusky" are crossed out in blue ink. One may infer that the unidentified "town facing Lake Michigan" may have been in Anderson's imagination much like the Ohio city of Sandusky which faces Lake Erie.

239:21   MS₁ (p. 156) reads: "... against soft gray unyielding walls."

242:7   In MS₁ (p. 158) SA uses "he" not "one."

244:11   Correctly spelled "dignity" in MS₁ (p. 159).

253:16   In MS₁ (p. 163) spelled "gayly." No correction is made on the manuscript.

254:1   Staining and fading of the manuscript make it impossible to read any revision, but the original type script of the sentence reads: "... and sleep beside Mary Webster in the days ..." MS₁ (p. 166).

255:10   Spelled "Natalia" in MS₁ (p. 167). SA consistently spelled the name "Natalia," but a Huebsch editor or printer apparently changed the spelling to "Natalie."

255:25   Not hyphenated in MS₁ (p. 167).

259:3   In MS₁ (p. 169) the sentence concludes: "... come such fool thing as he and Natalia were now doing."

BOOK REVIEWS OF <u>MANY MARRIAGES</u>

Boynton, H. W. <u>Independent</u>, 110 (31 March 1923), p. 232.

Broun, Heywood. <u>New York World</u> (25 February 1923), Section E, p. 6.

Canby, Henry S. <u>New York Evening Post Literary Review</u> (24 February 1923), p. 483.

Gould, Gerald. <u>Saturday Review</u>, 136 (8 September 1923), p. 281.

Jones, Llewellyn. <u>Chicago Evening Post Literary Review</u> (2 March 1923).

Lewisohn, Ludwig. <u>Nation</u>, 116 (28 March 1923), p. 368.

Littell, Robert. <u>New Republic</u>, 37 (11 April 1923), pp. 6-8.

Mencken, H. L. <u>Smart Set</u>, 71 (July 1923), pp. 138-39.

<u>New York Times Book Review</u> (25 February 1923), p. 10.

Rascoe, Burton. <u>New York Tribune Book News and Reviews</u> (25 February 1923), p. 17.

Stone, Percy N. <u>Bookman</u>, 57 (April 1923), pp. 210-11.

Wilson, Edmund. <u>Dial</u>, 74 (April 1923), pp. 399-400.

PS   137105   N4
3501   M25
DATE DUE   1978

DEMCO 25-370